AF345848

etiquette of spiritual
companionship

Etiquette of Spiritual Companionship

Mohamed Jedoui

Translated by
Ouiam al-Karkari &
Mohamed Lamine Dhokkar

Edited by
Marouen Jedoui

L·| LES 7 LECTURES

Etiquette of Spiritual Companionship
is published by the nonprofit organization Anwar
and his publishing house Les 7 Lectures

44 Fernand Brunfaut Street
1080 Brussels, Belgium

© Les 7 Lectures, 2024
All rights reserved

ISBN: 978-2-931274-01-9
Deposit number: D/2024/14.291/10 (Belgium)
Legal Deposit: January 2025

بسم الله الرحمن الرحيم
والصلاة والسلام على أشرف المرسلين
وعلى آله وأصحابه أجمعين

Table of Contents

To Mawlānā Shaykh, the ink of our pen.

Our parents, the crafters of our imprints.

Lillā Ouiam al-Karkari, our support.

*Sīdī Mohamed Lamine Dhokkar,
who translated for us.*

*Sīdī Abdul Hamid al-Zubdi,
the editor of our book.*

Preface

In the name of Allāh,
the Most Merciful, the Most Compassionate.

Praise be to Allāh, who has prepared His chosen ones for His divine presence with noble *ādāb*, and peace and blessings be upon our master Muḥammad, the one with the most exalted character, and upon his family and companions, who possess abundant virtues.

As soon as I read this book by my brother Dr. Mohamed Jedoui—may Allāh protect him—upon his kind invitation, I realized the importance of this rich addition to the library of the noble *Ṭarīqa Karkariyya*. Its significance stems from two main sources. First, the subject of the book revolves around the manners (*ādāb*) that the sufi seeker (*murīd*) should embody, both outwardly and inwardly, in his companionship with his Shaykh and guide on his journey to know his Lord, Almighty.

Secondly, the book draws from the living experience of the author in the companionship of the Shaykh of our age, Sīdī Mohamed Faouzi al-Karkari—may Allāh sanctify his secret.

Undoubtedly, proper *ādāb* is the most essential thing to seek and acquire before pursuing knowledge, as it serves as the compass for correct orientation and the vessel for navigating beneficial knowledge, leading to sound understanding and righteous action. ʿAbdullāh ibn al-Mubārak—may Allāh have mercy on him—said: "A person does not become virtuous by acquiring a particular type of knowledge unless they adorn that knowledge with *ādāb*."

Whoever becomes saturated with knowledge but devoid of *ādāb*, his knowledge will become a burden upon him, and expulsion and deprivation will be his condition.

Regarding this, Ibn Salām—may Allāh have mercy on him—said: "I stretched my legs towards the Kaʿba, and a woman came to me and said: 'You are from the people of knowledge, so do not sit without *ādāb*, or your name will be erased from the register of nearness (*dīwān al-qurb*).'"

For this reason, we find that the early scholars and virtuous people—according to the transmitted traditions and reports—paid great attention to acquiring good manners, making it their ultimate goal, and expending their most valuable years in this pursuit.

'Umar ibn al-Khaṭṭāb—may Allāh be pleased with him—said: "Learn *ādāb* before seeking knowledge."

This was the pedagogy followed by the Companions—may Allāh be pleased with them—which they inherited from the Greatest Educator, the Prophet ﷺ. As Ibn Sīrīn—may Allāh have mercy on him—said: "They used to learn guidance (*al-hadīy*) just as they learned knowledge."

This pedagogy continued in those who followed them. 'Abdullāh ibn al-Mubārak—may Allāh have mercy on him—said: "I sought *ādāb* for thirty years, and I sought knowledge for twenty years, and [the previous generations] used to seek *ādāb* before knowledge."

Al-Ḥasan al-Baṣrī—may Allāh have mercy on him—said: "A man would go out to refine his character for two years, then for two more years."

If this is the importance of *ādāb* for the seeker of outward knowledge, then its significance in the pursuit of spiritual knowledge—or what may be called the knowledge of *iḥsān*, or commonly referred to as the knowledge of Sufism—is even greater and more crucial.

Ādāb are a prerequisite for the fruition of acquired knowledge, not for its acquisition. How many scholars of the 'tongue' are there who lack *ādāb*? As for the knowledge of *iḥsān*, it cannot be attained or bear fruit except through *ādāb*.

Muḥammad ibn ʿAlī ibn Jaʿfar al-Kattānī—may Allāh have mercy on him—said: "Sufism is good character; whoever surpasses you in good character has surpassed you in Sufism."

For this reason, the people of Allāh placed great importance on *ādāb* and authored many books on the subject to help seekers on the path of proper conduct and true companionship. Among these are *The Etiquette of the Sufis* by Abū al-Qāsim al-Qushayrī—may Allāh have mercy on him—and *The Compendium of Sufi Etiquette* by Abū ʿAbd al-Raḥmān al-Sulamī—may Allāh have mercy on him—leading up to *The Pleasing Manners for the Sufi Path* by Muḥammad ibn Aḥmad al-Būzīdī—may Allāh have mercy on him. This latter book is given great attention in the *Ṭarīqa Karkariyya*, as recommended by our guiding Shaykh, Sīdī Mohamed Faouzi al-Karkari—may Allāh sanctify his secret.

Thus, the book before us follows the tradition of those who came before, offering a concise guide for seekers of Allāh's Face, drawn from the author's personal experiences in the company of the Shaykh—

may Allāh be pleased with him. It takes the reader on an educational journey, beginning with the correction and purification of intention and purpose, progressing through the path of love by embracing truthfulness and renouncing false claims, leading into the realm of *khidma* (service) and *da'wa* (preaching) guided by a wise approach that centers on the Prophetic Sunnah as mirrored by sainthood (*wilāya*), and ultimately raising the seeker to the heights of self-sacrifice, as Allāh says: **Indeed, Allāh has purchased from the believers their lives and their properties [in exchange] for that they will have Paradise.**[1]

Since these manners are meant to lead you to your concealed treasure, depending on your Lord's prescribed pre-eternal bounty and the share allocated to you by your Shaykh, the author concludes his book with two great set of *ādāb* that protect this treasure and preserve this station, guarding against its loss. We ask Allāh for safety!

It is appropriate for me and for those who read this book to study it carefully and draw from its depths with the intention of acting upon it, not merely to fill one's mind. The path is action and wayfaring; words alone do not suffice unless accompanied by deeds.

....

1   *Sūra 9. At-Tawba,* verse 111.

May Allāh grant us and you success in what He loves and is pleased with, and may He reward the author with the best reward for his work, by the blessing of the Shaykh, Sīdī Mohamed Faouzi al-Karkari—may Allāh sanctify his secret.[2]

Written by the humble servant of his Lord:
Abdul Hamid ibn Mohamed al-Zubdi.

....

2   We also extend our heartfelt gratitude to Dorra Jedoui and Mohamed Faouzi William Horner for their unwavering support and invaluable contributions to this book.

Introduction

I put my trust in Allāh and seek His protection from Satan. In the name of Allāh, the Most Gracious, the Most Merciful.

Praise be to Allāh, the Originator of the heavens and the earth, the Exalted above the '*Arsh*[3] and the *Kursī*[4] in the highest stations. He is the Light of every light, the Destroyer of the despots, and the Protector of the pious.

Peace and blessings be upon the noblest of creation, our master Muḥammad, the Trustworthy, and upon his manifestations, the elite of his revered progeny. He is the manifestation of perfection, the mercy of the Exalted, the reviver of the impossible, the elixir of beauty, and the softener of majesty. He is the intercessor whose intercession is accepted, the exalted and elevated, humble and devout, the secret

....

3   The Throne of God.
4   The Pedestal.

of all secrets and the source of all lights, the beloved and the lover, the seeker and the sought. None can encompass his worth except the Existent, and none knows his true right except the Worshiped.

And peace and blessings be upon the prophets of Allāh, His messengers, the blessed companions, the chosen family of the Prophet and upon every righteous one. Amen.

Indeed, we have compiled this book before you with the blessing and permission of our Shaykh and Master, Sīdī Mohamed Faouzi al-Karkari—may Allāh sanctify his noble secret. It is a summary of the teachings we received in his companionship and during our time in his flourishing *zāwiya* (sufi lodge) in the Sharifian Kingdom of Morocco for more than two years. He is the greatest Shaykh, the most honored *walī* (Friend of Allāh), the eternal seal of realization, and the noblest in lineage and spirit on every path. He is the perfect and complete one, the jewel of existence, through whose radiant light Allāh dispelled the darkness of tyranny, and by whose powerful breath (*nafas*), the dead were brought to life.

He says—may Allāh sanctify his noble secret—in one of his aphorisms: "The bowing of encompassing knowledge is a sign of uprightness and proper etiquette for the one who recognizes the true value of the dot. But for the one who is ignorant of its worth, their bowing becomes crooked, and their water turns bitter. **They have not appraised Allāh with true appraisal.**[5]

Indeed, the path to the Intermediated (*mawsūṭ*) is firmly tied to maintaining unconditioned etiquette (*ādāb*) with the intermediary (*wāsiṭa*). However, for the one who neglects proper *ādāb* with him, their path leads to hellfire, and their journey becomes one of misery and bitterness.

O Allāh, by the secret of Your bestowed mercy, make this work solely for Your noble countenance. Illuminate our hearts through it, and by the rank of Your *walī*, remove from it all manifest deviation. Peace and blessings be upon the best of creation, our master Muḥammad, the noble-hearted, and upon his family, companions, and all those who follow them in goodness, from the beginning to the end.

----

5   *Sūra 6. Al-Anʿām*, verse 91.

Brief Biography

Al-Khatm Shyakh Mohamed Faouzi al-Karkari
In the name of Allāh, the Most Gracious, the Most Merciful. Complete and perfect blessings and peace be upon our master Muḥammad, the light of creation, and upon his pure and noble family, the full moons, and his pious companions, the ancient stars.

This is a humble attempt by one unworthy of approaching the divine presence to narrate the life of the one closest to divine subsistence, the noble, pure, and dignified Sīdī Mohamed Faouzi al-Karkari—may Allāh sanctify his noble secret. He is a descendant of the House of Prophethood, from the branch of the master (*mawlā*) of the world and religion, the grandson of the leader of the messengers, the son of the flower of the worlds (i.e. Sayyida Fātima), from the lineage of the lion of religion, Sayyidunā al-Ḥasan, the epitome of beauty—upon whom, and upon all of them, be peace and blessings.

He—may Allāh be pleased with him—was born at dawn on Wednesday, the second of July, 1974, corresponding to the twelfth of Jumādā al-Thānī, 1394, in the northern part of the land of the Sharīfs, the source of saints, the kingdom of the pious, the Maghreb of Islam, the land of scholars, particularly in the Rif region. He comes from a Sharifian lineage with origins firmly rooted in the land of prophethood and messengerhood, with branches reaching high into the sky of sainthood, continuously bearing fruit and manifesting divine grace in every era. Among his most famous ancestors is Mawlānā Ibn Qaddūr al-Wakīlī, the fifth grandfather of our Shaykh—may Allāh sanctify his noble secret—who informed his family and kin of Sīdī Shaykh's future role as the greatest Seal (*al-khatm*) before he returned to his Lord's presence. He is the son of Mawlānā al-Ṭayyib, son of Mawlānā al-Ṭāhir, son of Mawlānā al-Fardī, son of Mawlānā Ibn Qaddūr al-Wakīlī from his father's side. As for his mother's side, he is the son of Lallā Yāmna, daughter of Mawlānā al-Ṭayyib, son of Mawlānā al-Fardī, son of Mawlānā Ibn Qaddūr al-Wakīlī—may Allāh be pleased with them all.

Our Shaykh—may Allāh sanctify his noble secret—was beloved by his grandfather, our valiant master al-Ṭāhir, the inheritor of the secret of Mawlānā al-Alāwī—may Allāh be pleased with both of them.

He confirmed in him the news foretold by his grand-father (i.e., Ibn Qaddūr) regarding his high spiritual resolve (*himma*) and informed both those near and far of the rise of his spiritual sun.

However, like every great *walī*, his life began with trials. From childhood onwards, he faced the most dangerous conspiracies, carried out by those closest to him. He sacrificed his youth and left his home, wandering in the land of his Lord, seeking death from his *nafs* and the slander that had been cast upon him.

He wandered for ten full years, during which he encountered people of all ranks, both elite and common, and studied the sciences of signs and manifestations in the horizons of his Lord. Speaking about his wandering (*siyāḥa*), he tells us—may Allāh sanctify his noble secret: "I did not embark on this journey except in search of death, after the horizons became too narrow for me due to the bitterness of the slander I endured."

He also says—may Allāh sanctify his noble secret: "In my *siyāḥa*, I tasted true freedom and fully experienced the reality of reliance (*tawakkul*) on the Lord of creation. No one can teach me about this matter; if I was hungry, the Lord would send me food; and if I was tired, I would lay down on the ground and sleep under His watchful eye. Stones and trees would speak to me and keep me company, while I felt uneasy in the presence of other human beings. I witnessed the reality of mercy in those whom people consider the lowest of creation, and the horizons taught me never to judge others, regardless of their path. The judgment of the eye is false when it comes to inward realities, and what you perceive as the torment of Hell may, by the will of the Lord of the worlds, be the paradise of mercy for many of His servants."

After ten years of wandering, his Lord called him back through a vision to return to his hometown. In 2005, he returned to his birthplace and reunited with the most beloved person in his heart, his pure and chaste mother, Lallā Yāmna—may Allāh have mercy on her. This had been his only prayer during his wandering—to see her again before she returned to her Lord.

The most significant moment upon his return to his birthplace was his meeting with his Shaykh, Mawlānā al-Ḥasan ibn al-Ṭāhir, his uncle—may Allāh be pleased with both of them—who inherited the secret of his father in guiding people to Allāh. He recognized in him the only door to repentance from himself and the burdens that had clung to him since his childhood trials. Stripping himself of everything from his past, he donned the robe of reliance on Allāh and set out barefoot toward his Shaykh's door in the direction of Temsamane (Driouch Province). Along the journey, the light of his Lord shone upon him, and he walked towards his Shaykh weeping, humble, and repentant, despite the distance of more than seventy kilometers.

He tells us—may Allāh sanctify his noble secret: "I had stripped myself of everything I owned and gave away every garment I wore, leaving only a robe to cover myself. I saw in Mawlānā al-Ḥasan the only door to the acceptance of my repentance from the bitterness I endured in my childhood. I walked, weeping, humble, and burdened by my Lord. As soon as I took the road to Temsamane, a light began to shine before me—a sun that outshone the midday sun. I thought I had gone blind, as I could no longer see ahead or behind me, but the weight of repentance in my heart prevented me from focusing on this state. I continued walking, even as my feet stepped on thorns, without caring. When I reached my uncle's house, my only concern was that he would open the door of repentance for me from what had clung to me from my childhood trials. At first, he rejected me, closing his door to test my intention. When I saw this rejection, I said to him, 'If you do not accept me, I will return to my wandering, hoping to find the acceptance of my Lord in other horizons.' He was pleased with me and my firmness of purpose. He instructed his noble daughter—may Allāh be pleased with both of them—to prepare the place of seclusion (*khulwa*) for me, promising that Allāh would accept my repentance in it."

Mawlānā al-Ḥasan—may Allāh be pleased with him—placed Sīdī Shaykh in the blessed seclusion at the beginning of the month of Shawwāl that year, instructing him not to sleep during it, to fast from food and drink, to remain devoted to obligatory prayers, and to engage in the remembrance of the Supreme Name, Allāh. The first night passed, and the Shaykh visited him the next morning to see what spiritual openings his nephew—may Allāh be pleased with both of them—had experienced. He told him that he had not seen anything the previous night that would indicate the acceptance of his repentance or bring comfort to his soul. The Shaykh realized that he had not engaged in the remembrance of the Supreme Name but had only persisted in seeking forgiveness. When asked why he had not followed the instruction to remember the Name, he replied, "I seek only the acceptance of my repentance and my Lord's forgiveness. This is my sole hope in life." Mawlānā al-Ḥasan—may Allāh be pleased with him—responded: "My son, know that the Supreme Name of Allāh encompasses all forms of remembrance, including seeking forgiveness and repentance. Follow my instruction, and you will witness the proof of your repentance."

On the second night, Mawlānā Shaykh—may Allāh sanctify his noble secret—was granted the station of the Seal (*al-khatmīya*). Through divine manifestation (*tajallī*) and embodiment (*taḥallī*), he grasped the secret of Divinity and ascended with both body and spirit to the Lote Tree of Sainthood, drinking from the degrees of the secret with understanding and mastery. He comprehended the reality of his past and present, and he foresaw what awaited him in the future as the inevitable guide to his Lord.

One remarkable event during his seclusion on the second night and what followed was that, through the remembrance (*dhikr*) of the Supreme Name, he would wander with body and soul in the universe of his Lord, unaware of his physical surroundings. When Mawlānā al-Ḥasan—may Allāh be pleased with him—came to check on him, he did not find him in the seclusion. Astonished, he searched everywhere but could not locate him. After some time, he returned to the seclusion and found him there. He asked, "What took you out of here, my son?" He replied that he had not left but had been sitting in his place the entire time. Mawlānā al-Ḥasan realized the high station Sīdī Shaykh—may Allāh be pleased with him—had attained and began explaining to him the manifestations of the Supreme Name that had been revealed to him. Mawlānā Shaykh—may Allāh sanctify his noble secret—would see the Name manifest with all that came from it and immediately understand it through the verses of the Qur'ān. Indeed, he drank from the ocean of divine knowledge and all it contained.

He continued his seclusion for three nights. On the final day, Mawlānā al-Ḥasan came to give him permission to return to the *julwa* (public space), but he refused to leave the seclusion (*khulwa*), saying, "Here I found my Lord; what need do I have for the *julwa*?" Mawlānā al-Ḥasan—may Allāh be pleased with him—explained that he was now walking with the secret of his Lord, so his *julwa* had become his *khulwa*. As Allāh says: **wherever you turn, there is the Face of Allāh.**[6]

Mawlānā al-Ḥasan—may Allāh be pleased with him—would often remind his family and kin that his nephew—may Allāh sanctify his noble secret—was among the greatest of Saints. After the passing of his uncle—may Allāh be pleased with him—the secret returned to Mawlānā Shaykh—may Allāh sanctify his secret—and he inherited the Shaykh's authority (*al-Mashyakha*). During his uncle's illness, he would pray to the Lord to take his soul and spare his Shaykh, hoping that others would continue to benefit from

....

6   *Sūra 2. Al-Baqara*, verse 115.

him. For Mawlānā Shaykh—may Allāh sanctify his noble secret—never saw himself as having any existence apart from his Shaykh, and he saw no benefit in himself due to his complete self-annihilation in him.

However, Allāh willed to renew His mercy within His creation and to raise from the Ummah of His Prophet, peace and blessings be upon him and his family, one who would revive the command of religion and restore its clarity to the people. The command (*al-amr*) and permission (*al-ʾidhn*) to call people to Allāh and guide them to Him came to our Shaykh directly from our master, the Messenger of Allāh, peace and blessings be upon him and his family, and from the Lord of Glory, the Exalted.

Thus, the light of Allāh began to flow through the people at the hands of Mawlānā Shaykh—may Allāh sanctify his noble secret—and the lamps of believers were kindled with his clear light from all corners of the world. Despite campaigns of slander, doubt, and enmity from both near and far, his *ṭarīqa* (path) spread rapidly, captivating both noble Arabs and non-Arabs alike. Since 2007, every soul longing for its true homeland has made pilgrimage to him, and by the blessing of his supplication, all hearts seeking their Lord have been ignited. His miracles filled the world, and people came to him on foot from the lands of both Arabs and Westerners. He chose to sacrifice his own comfort and that of his family for the sake of educating those who seek Allāh. He settled his family in his *zāwiya* and opened himself to all who desired to draw near to Allāh.

We have not found in the history of divinely-guided Shaykhs a path that grants spiritual openings as swiftly as his, nor have we read in books or traditions of disciples as numerous as those on his path. Thousands have witnessed his miracles. Through commitment to him (*bayʿa*), the knowledge of Allāh, His angels, His books, and His messengers—upon them and our Prophet be peace and blessings—has been revived in both manifestation (*tajallī*) and meaning (*maʿnā*). The Lord of Glory and the Prophet of Mercy, peace and blessings be upon him and his family, have directed people toward him through visions and dreams. His light shines, at midday and in every state, upon his disciples.

Allāh clothed him in the character of the Merciful, making him a tree that illuminates every sinful and longing soul. He is merciful to all people, always smiling, bringing joy, and loving simplicity. He is gentle and light like a breeze, compassionate and merciful to all beings. He loves those who are easygoing and who make things easy for others, quick to laugh and quick to shed tears. He dislikes artificiality and those who 'wear masks', but he loves the truthful, even if they are immersed in sin. Constantly engaged in remembrance, he never parts from his litanies and cherishes the night, standing in prayer during the pre-dawn hours. During the time of the coronavirus pandemic, we would spend the nights with him—may Allāh sanctify his noble secret—in remembrance and supplication. When he sat in the *miḥrāb* to engage in *dhikr*, he would not leave his place until the hour of pre-dawn remembrance arrived, even in the winter season. Allāh tested him with us, and we did not fully comprehend the reality of his station. Yet, the more we increased in our transgressions, the more his compassion and mercy towards us in our ignorance grew.

His spiritual education (*tarbiya*) is the beauty of beauties (*jamāl al-jamāl*), and his blessing (*baraka*) has lifted from us the majesty (*jalāl*) of divine connection (*wiṣāl*). He continuously holds lessons in his *zāwiya*, attended by hundreds of disciples, both privately and publicly. All his words are imbued with deep meaning, effortlessly drawing from the secret of Allāh. Those unfamiliar with him are astonished by his quick, profound, and clear interpretation of visions, the *ḥadīths* of the Prophet, peace and blessings be upon him, and the verses of the Qur'ān.

The foolish and shameless waged war against him, while the humble among religious and secular scholars followed him. Those closest to him were tested by their opposition to him, and the wicked even went so far as to poison him in an attempt to make him suffer. Yet, this only deepened his attachment and love for Allāh, and Allāh exposed the ill intentions of those who sought to harm him, revealing them to both near and distant.

Those who listened to his advice and acted upon it immediately were successful, while those who engaged in excessive questioning and conversation with him lost out. He reveals everything concealed with just a few words and shows you the outcome of your orientation, even if you did not ask about it.

We saw him, after being poisoned, carrying the weight of majesty on his shoulders without complaint or concern for his own condition. He loved us with the love of Allāh and His Messenger, peace and blessings be upon him and his family, and he never misled any of us in advice or guidance. Due to his high station with the Lord, he planted in the hearts of his disciples secrets that baffle the mind. He has authored works in the spiritual sciences that bewilder the intellect, and those who humble themselves before Allāh, no matter who they are, submit to him and recognize his sainthood.

The mind withdraws in awe before his love for Allāh and His chosen ones, peace be upon them. His proximity is a cure for spiritual distance and a hammer for the rust of hearts and for all who are blind.

May Allāh benefit us through him in every state and utterance, and may Allāh annihilate us in him so that we see nothing of ourselves except his constant breath. O Allāh, in conclusion, send prayers and firm salutations upon our master Muḥammad, the root of the tree of the blessed family, upon his family, his heirs who lead to the truth of the Qurʾān, and his companions, the stars of guidance in the sky of illumination, and upon all who follow them consistently in goodness; so that we may be saved from the deviations of denial, the darkness of wickedness, and the confusion of the evildoers.

I.

Intention in the *Bay'a* (Commitment)

Allāh Almighty says: **Say, whether you conceal what is in your hearts or reveal it, it is known to Allāh.**[7]

Know, may Allāh, His Messenger, and His *walī* guide us to the clear path, that Allāh Almighty is fully aware of the intentions of His servants, knowledgeable of their innermost secrets, and encompassing of their outward actions.

Be certain of this: Allāh and His *walī* are exalted above us, possessing greater knowledge. And know, without doubt, that Allāh granted His Beloved, upon whom be peace and blessings, the ability to see with His sight, as the Lord of Glory said through the tongue of the Prophet of Mercy, peace and blessings be upon him: "I become his sight with which he sees."

....

7   *Sūra* 3. *Āl-'Imrān*, verse 29.

And as the Messenger of Allāh ﷺ said: "Beware of the insight (*firāsa*) of the believer, for indeed he sees with the light of Allāh."[8]

The Beloved, Almighty, does not conceal anything from His beloved—the believer embodying the secret of the *alif lām* (definite article) of definition, the illuminated *walī* from the noble family—what is hidden in the hearts through divine arrangement.

Know, while keeping in mind that Allāh and His Messenger, peace and blessings be upon him, are more knowledgeable and higher than me and you, that the difference between a believer and a hypocrite lies in their acceptance that what is concealed is manifest to Allāh and His Beloved, peace and blessings be upon him and his family.

Indeed, the Prophet, peace and blessings be upon him, was fully aware of the heart of every hypocrite and knew the rank of every elevated believer. He gave glad tidings of Paradise to ten of his closest companions and warned the group of hypocrites about the Fire.

So, do not pretend before the Judge to possess qualities you do not truly have. The first step in understanding this is to be truthful with the *walī* of

....

8   Al-Tirmidhī, *Sunan al-Tirmidhī, Kitāb Tafsīr al-Qur'ān* (*The Book of Exegesis*), *ḥadīth* 3127.

the time about the intentions concealed in your heart so that he may guide them toward facing solely the sacred sanctuary. Intention (*niyya*) is the secret key to entering the Divine Presence. Its purity is inextricably linked to acknowledging its shortcomings when seeking guidance from the *Khalīfa* of the Most Merciful so that He may take your hand and guide you toward the exalted stations of *Iḥsān*.

A. The *walī* Leads You towards Sincere Repentance

Let your intention, O seeker of the Divine Presence, be that the *walī* takes you by the hand and leads you to Allāh, affirming for you a sincere repentance from the inclinations that prevent you from turning to Him with full sincerity. For when you and I come to the path, we are in the depths of the turbulent sea of the self, stained with the impurities of devils—pride, vanity, and envy—known only to the manifest *imām*. Allāh has concealed these from us out of mercy, for if the veil of our heedlessness regarding our true selves were lifted all at once, we would be struck with a deadly shock of terror.

So, do not claim that you have come as a repentant, for this is a statement whose reality you do not truly understand, and it is closer to arrogance than to the truth, except for those whom the Lord of Creation has shown mercy. The Almighty says through the words of the prophet Yūsuf (Joseph)—peace be upon him: **And I do not seek to absolve my *nafs* from blame, for indeed the nafs is ever inclined to evil, except those shown mercy by my Lord. Surely my Lord is All-Forgiving, Most Merciful.**[9] This is your master and mine, Yūsuf the Truthful, the protected and trustworthy, whom the Lord of the worlds has purified. He does not dare to attribute to himself the qualities of the perfected repentants, nor does he absolve his self from the tendency toward evil. So what about our state, we who are but poor souls?

The true repentant is the one who has reached the Almighty, whose lower self, the blaming soul, and the inspired soul have all died, and whose soul has become tranquil through Allāh. O Allāh, join us with them. Whoever claims this station in their pledge to Allāh will be passed through the reality of repentance by Allāh and tested on their false claim. The veil of protection will be stripped away, exposing them before their peers, revealing that they are a servant of the lower self, not a servant of Allāh.

Such a person then seizes the rights of their brothers, causes discord among peers, and everyone complains of their aggression, while they themselves complain about others without any real cause or evidence.

....

9   *Sūra 12. Yūsuf*, verse 53.

They cannot refrain from anger, do not consider the state of those closest to them, and fail to acknowledge the defects within themselves.

However, the true repentant has a soul that has died and now flows through Allāh. They see no evil in the universe and look only at the Reckoner with the eye of the Most Merciful. Their soul has died to fluctuations and has been annihilated in the reality of divine manifestations. If you insult them, they forgive you; if you take their rights, they thank you. They have repented from all and everything, wandering solely in the Presence of the One. They are not affected by the transient, but through them, destinies are affected. They are the image of the Most Merciful, the blessing of their time and era, without equal among beings, a nectar from the elite of the lineage of the noble Prophet, peace and blessings be upon him and his family.

Thus, if the claimant of this station, lacking clear evidence, were among the graced ones, he would awaken from his ignorance, reflect on himself, reconsider his supposed repentance, acknowledge his own shortcomings, and understand the danger of speaking without clear proof. But if he is among the people of aggression, he would depart from the path that he never truly entered into, in reality (taḥqīq), except for God to reveal the truth of his hypocrisy among his peers.

Therefore, always remember, before approaching the *imām*, the corruption you have caused in the universe, so that your tyrant *nafs* realizes it is poison, deceitful, and far from the Most Merciful, and that your claim to perfection is nothing but a lie to others.

Remember the injustices you have committed and the rights you have yet to restore. If you find nothing, close your eyes and confront the darkness of your spiritual night, contemplating the blackness of your guilty soul, as our Shaykh often advises. If you still claim righteousness, remember that, according to the *ḥadīth* of the Prophet, in this darkness, you see the reality of your grave—a dreadful, dark abyss. The Prophet, peace be upon him, said: "The grave is like a piece of the darkest night. O people, if you knew what I know, you would weep much and laugh little. O people, seek refuge in Allāh from the torment of the grave, for indeed the torment of the grave is true."[10]

Therefore, fear yourself, accuse it, and acknowledge that it is distant from the Divine, even if you haven't yet tasted this truth. Seek refuge in Allāh from it. Before committing to the healer of souls (*nufūs*), be cautious, for if he uncovers the vessel for you, you may fall into the pit of false claims.

....

10 Al-Bukhārī, *Ṣaḥīḥ al-Bukhārī, Kitāb al-Jana'iz* (*The Book of Funerals*), *ḥadīth* 1372.

If you intend for the *walī* to guide you to the Most Merciful, the path becomes easy for you. His kindness will surround you in every difficulty and distress, gently guiding you through the stages of realization, because you have not claimed what is not within you and have approached him with humility, fleeing from the language of embellishment.

Do not pretend righteousness before him; instead, acknowledge that you are not among the people of righteousness until he makes you one of them. What need do you have for a Shaykh if you are already righteous and successful?

But if you recognize your unworthiness, he will be the one to refine you. If you know you are not successful, he will guide you to success. If you know you are a hypocrite, he will lead you to truthfulness. If you know you are distant, he will bring you closer. If you know you are in darkness, he will purify you. Indeed, it is through opposites that things are recognized. However, if you claim righteousness and take *bay'a*, it becomes incumbent upon Allāh to reveal, through the stick of the *walī*, your darkness to the world—so prepare yourself for trials.

B. Migration to Allāh, not to Anyone else

The Prophet Muḥammad ﷺ said: "Actions are judged by intentions, and every person will have only what they intended. So, whoever's migration was for Allāh and His Messenger, their migration was indeed for Allāh and His Messenger. And whoever's migration was for some worldly gain or to marry a woman, their migration was for whatever purpose they migrated."[11]

Whoever approaches the *imām* with intentions that deviate from seeking the Knowledge of Allāh and being guided to the Most Merciful will inevitably go astray. If your purpose is worldly—be it marriage, work, healing, or any other mundane intention—do not present yourself under the guise of *īmān*, pretending to come for the sake of the Most Merciful. Instead, reveal your true intentions and confess them to your Shaykh. Only then can he correct your shortcomings and properly prepare you for the *bayʿa*.

As for the one who conceals his true intentions, as soon as the *walī* takes his hand, the universe will strip him 'naked' before everyone, exposing his vice and revealing his lie. Our Shaykh—may Allāh sanctify his secret—has said: "Whoever comes to us and lies about his intention during *bayʿa*, Allāh will expose him within forty days."

....

11 Al-Bukhārī, *Ṣaḥīḥ al-Bukhārī, Kitāb al-Īmān* (*The Book of Faith*), *ḥadīth* 1.

It is crucial for those who seek to reach the Divine Presence to carefully study the conditions for embarking on the journey with the divinely connected righteous *walī*. Through this preparation, one gains insight into their own self and the true aim of their heart when placing their foot in the presence of the Cupbearer (*as-sāqī*), i.e., the Shaykh. One should not approach impulsively, driven by a fleeting desire for discovery or a wish for seclusion to escape worldly troubles. Indeed, this station is not an ordinary one; it is the holy assembly (*ḥaḍra*) of the intermediate world, subsisting between the highest heavens and the lowest earths—a great, noble, powerful, and dangerous station, crowned with the holder of the secret of transcendence (*tanzīh*) in the realm of comparability (*tashbīh*) without a comparable (*shabīh*). It is the gateway to salvation for those who revere it, and a path to downfall for those who belittle it.

C. Refrain from Saying, "I Came for the Sake of Allāh (*lillāh*)"

Whoever comes for the sake of Allāh becomes a reflection of the double *lām* and the *hāʾ*, embodying thirty degrees from the stations of the Supreme Name. But how can this be for someone whose soul has been veiled from Allāh throughout his life, yet claims that he came for the sake of Allāh (*lillāh*)? It is more fitting for those like us, who are mired in heedlessness, not to claim what we do not truly understand. Instead, we should allow the Beloved of the Most Merciful to construct a path for us to know the Lord, guiding us through the stations of excellence (*al-iḥsān*) according to our capacity. This is the essence of the intention to migrate to the Bountiful (*al-mannān*)—recognizing that we are outside the circle of true recognition and seeking our Shaykh's guidance to illuminate a path for us with a ray of His light. Through this, we may traverse the degrees of the Name with the blessed breath (*nafās*) of al-Adnān, peace and blessings be upon him.

But for the one who insists and says, "I came for the sake of Allāh", claiming the station of the righteous, he must be sure that such a claim will not go untested. Woe to the one who fails the test due to his tongue, which does not hesitate to lie to the Vicegerent (*khalīfa*) of the Most Merciful.

The Prophet Muḥammad ﷺ said: "Whoever guarantees me what is between his jaws and what is between his legs, I guarantee him Paradise." So, do not claim what you do not possess or persist in professing it with your tongue, for such actions may obstruct your path to Allāh and lead you towards the fires of Hell. Abū Bakr al-Ṣiddīq —may Allāh be pleased with him—often lived by this verse:

Beware of your tongue,
lest you say something and be tested,
for indeed, trials are assigned to one's speech.[12]

12 Ibn al-Qayyim, *Tuḥfat al-Mawdūd*, p. 123.

II.

The Issue of Love: "I Love You, O Shaykh!"

Muḥammad al-Mahdī al-Fāsī al-Qaṣrī reports: "The Prophet Muḥammad ﷺ said, 'None of you truly believes until I am more beloved to him than himself, his wealth, his children, his parents, and all people.' This is also confirmed in the *ḥadīth* of ʿUmar ibn al-Khaṭṭāb—may Allāh be pleased with him—as narrated by al-Bukhārī from ʿAbdullāh ibn Hishām—may Allāh be pleased with him. ʿUmar said to the Prophet Muḥammad ﷺ, 'O Messenger of Allāh, you are dearer to me than everything except my own self.' The Prophet ﷺ replied, 'No, by Him in Whose Hand my soul is, your faith is not complete until I am dearer to you than your own self.' Then ʿUmar—may Allāh be pleased with him—said, 'Now, by Allāh, you are dearer to me than my own self.' The Prophet ﷺ then said, 'Now, O 'Umar, [your faith is complete.]'"[13]

If we were to connect these two *hadīths*, we would understand that the station of love is not merely a matter of words expressed by the disciple, but rather a profound sacrifice that is difficult to attain. It is like a sharp blade against the neck of one's inclinations, severing all attachments, even those deeply ingrained within oneself. This is akin to the sacrifice made by Sayyidunā Ibrāhīm, the *khalīl* of al-Raḥmān, who was willing to sacrifice his pure offspring, Sayyidunā Ismā'īl, peace be upon him. Are we truly prepared to sacrifice our wealth, our children, our parents, and even our very selves for the sake of the elite of the Prophet's progeny, peace and blessings be upon them?

Let us not deceive ourselves; we are weak, flawed, and driven by our desires. We lack true submission and possess little strength. When we are hungry, we waver in our faith; when we are in pain, we complain. We should not place ourselves among the ranks of the pure and devoted—in truth, we are the afflicted and the deluded. As our Shaykh—may Allāh sanctify his noble secret—often reminds us: "Do not tell me,

....

13 Al-Bukhārī, *Ṣaḥīḥ al-Bukhārī, Kitāb al-Īmān* (*The Book of Faith*), *ḥadīth* 6632 (*Book 78, ḥadīth 6684*).

'I love you, O Shaykh!' For love is sacrifice, not just words that flow from the tongue. With the letter *hā'* (ح), whose numerical value is eight, representing the eight angels who bear the Throne of the Most Merciful, and the letter *Bā'* (ب), whose numerical value is two, with its dot beneath the line from the depths of the *jabarūt* (The Realm of Divine Invincibility). When they are brought together, they yield ten—the complete annihilation of the zero into the One..."

Know for certain that you will never attain the station of "the Beloved" (*al-Ḥabīb*), for the Beloved is One without a partner—annihilated in Him, subsisting by Him, a realized form (*ṣūra*) for His divine manifestation. After the Prophet, peace be upon him, your Shaykh is the manifestation of "the Beloved" in our time. Do not presume to rival him in what Allāh has uniquely bestowed upon him. Rather, strive diligently in the path of Allāh through your words, by spreading the message; and through your deeds, by sacrificing your wealth and self, under the guidance of Allāh's *walī*. In this way, the *walī* may elevate you and me from the lowly station of hypocrites to become a pure reflection of the Beloved of all the Worlds, peace be upon him.

Never say "I love you", even if the *walī* says it to you, so that you do not elevate yourself to his lofty station or falsely purify what is not yet pure. Instead, pray that Allāh gently and beautifully (with *jamāl*) extinguishes you in the love of your Shaykh. Do not seek trials or majesty (*jalāl*), lest you fall into the fires of tribulation. Always be cautious of such claims, and remember that you came from a lowly fluid—humble, weak, and insignificant in origin.

As the verse says: **Allāh has indeed purchased from the believers their selves (*anfusahum*) and wealth in exchange for Paradise. They fight in the cause of Allāh and kill or are killed.**[14]

Have you sacrificed anything of this sort? Have you "killed" and "been killed"? Have you even asked yourself if you and I are among those capable of enduring such trials? The Messenger of Allāh ﷺ said: "Whoever believes in Allāh and the Last Day, let him speak good or remain silent." Indeed, in our silence on matters of such elevated stations lies virtue, and in our prayers for Allāh to refine us, there is true goodness.

We say, by the grace of Mawlānā Shaykh—may Allāh sanctify his noble secret—and his words take precedence over ours:

....

14 *Sūra* 9. *At-Tawba*, verse 111.

The Speech of Pronouns

Do not say "I love", for love cannot
originate from you,
You are death, darkness, evil,
heedlessness, and wrath.

Love originates from the Beloved,
who loved you first,
And revived His soul within you.

As for you, you are not fit for love.

Say instead, "I am the hateful, I am the hypocrite,
I am the foolish."

Say it first until you taste it.

For due to the intensity of your disobedience,
You cannot see it in yourself at the start.

And if you do see it in yourself,
it is not you who saw it,
Because seeing it is good, and good is from Allāh.

So say it, perhaps the Beloved
will reveal it to you.

Indeed, things are known through their opposites,
And so is love.

But even then, you will never truly know it,
For only the Beloved knows it.

Whatever good befalls you is from Allāh, and whatever evil befalls you is from your own self. We have sent you, [O Prophet,] as a messenger to all people, and Allāh is sufficient as a Witness.[15]

. . . .

15 *Sūra* 4. *An-Nisā'*, verse 79.

III.

The Companionship of the Shaykh

Allāh, the Exalted, says: **As for the foremost—the first of the Muhajirūn (those who migrated from Mecca to Medina) and the Ansār (the residents of Medina who supported them)—and those who follow them in goodness, Allāh is pleased with them, and they are pleased with Him. He has prepared for them Gardens beneath which rivers flow, where they will dwell forever. That is the supreme success.**[16]

Know, and Allāh, His Messenger, and His *walī* know better than you and I, that divine pleasure (*riḍā*) is reserved for those who are present, as Mawlānā Abū Shu'ayb al-Ghawth—may Allāh be pleased with him—said in his famous poem. There is no divine pleasure for those whose hearts are not in a state of presence before their bodies. Moreover,

....

16 *Sūra* 9. *At-Tawba*, verse 100.

the heart cannot be truly present without the body being fully present as well.

If a disciple's heart finds contentment in anything other than what his Shaykh has approved for him, he has strayed from the presence of true divine pleasure in what he is content with. Conversely, if a disciple's heart is aligned with what his Shaykh—may Allāh sanctify his noble secret—has approved, then Allāh is pleased with him and has prepared for him gardens of knowledge and blessings, both manifest and hidden, beneath which rivers of life flow eternally. This divine pleasure will remain as long as the disciple does not redirect his heart toward anything other than the one whom Allāh has approved—may Allāh sanctify his noble secret.

A. Never Associate any Partner with the Shaykh

Know, and Allāh knows best, that the companionship of the *faqīr* (spiritual seeker) with the Shaykh is the cornerstone of the spiritual journey. Whoever turns away from the Shaykh in this journey is, in essence, turning away from Allāh, and whoever turns towards the Shaykh is turning towards Allāh, for the Shaykh serves as the gateway to the Prophet ﷺ and the Prophet is the gateway to Allāh, the Almighty. These doors are interconnected, so neglecting the door of the Shaykh is tantamount to neglecting the subsequent doors that lead to the Divine. The Messenger of Allāh ﷺ said: "I am the city of knowledge, and ʿAlī is its gate. So, whoever seeks knowledge should come to the gate."[17]

Therefore, whoever seeks knowledge of the self should turn to the Shaykh and not to anyone else, as the Shaykh is the inheritor of that gate in his time. From the moment the *faqīr* enters the path, it is essential that he focuses solely on his Shaykh and refrains from taking advice from others. After all, how can someone lost in darkness offer guidance to the *faqīr*? How can the spiritually-ailing ones advise each other when they both seek healing for the same afflictions?

Indeed, when you enter the spiritual path, everything in creation can become a barrier between you and your Lord, except for your Shaykh, who alone can connect you to Allāh, the Almighty. When you come to the *zāwiya*, let your focus be solely on your Shaykh, and see no one else in his place. Wherever he sits, sit with him; wherever he travels, follow him. Always maintain the intention in your heart to learn from him, to be purified of your delusions through him, and to draw closer to Allāh by him. You did not travel to the *zāwiya* to hide from him—in fact,

---

17 Al-Suyuti, *Al-Jami' al-Saghir*, 2690.

what purpose would your presence serve if you kept yourself hidden?

As the Shaykh says: "If you come here to hide from me, then don't come at all—stay at home instead." The *zāwiya* is not just walls or a group of disciples; the *zāwiya* is your Shaykh. When you sit with him, he nurtures you, purifies you, and refines you, even if you are steeped in disobedience.

I was once sitting in the presence of our Shaykh—may his noble secret be sanctified—with my brother Sīdī Marouen—may Allāh preserve him. We were outside the *zāwiya* near the sheepfold, and our Shaykh said to us: "A disciple who distances himself from me may think he is maintaining high etiquette (*ādāb*), but in reality, he is only harming himself by staying away. When a disciple draws near to the Shaykh, the Shaykh corrects him, straightens him, and purifies him from lowly traits. The closer the disciple sits to the Shaykh, the more his inner 'serpents' are driven away. But the farther he is, the deeper those serpents embed themselves. If you come closer to me, I will reform you, but if you stay away, you will only harm yourself."

When you arrive at the *zāwiya*, do not view anyone as a partner with your Shaykh, and do not place any disciple or anyone else between you and him, for these are all veils that distance you from the purpose for which you came; that your Shaykh takes your hand and leads you to your Lord. This does not mean you should shun or be hostile to the disciples; on the contrary, as our Shaykh teaches, you should see them as better than yourself and recognize that it is you who may be an obstacle to them on the path. Withdraw from everything except your Shaykh, and in doing so, you will forge a path toward the knowledge of the One, the Absolute. You cannot truly know Him while you are immersed in numbers, multiplicity, and worldly distractions.

Remember, you did not enter the path until you realized you were unable to know God and reach Him through the creation that surrounded you. Simply put, whoever does not make the Shaykh his *qibla* in all things has no hope in the path to God.

B. Honesty Brings Peace

Be completely honest with your Shaykh about all the obstacles you encounter on your path to Allāh, whether they are spiritual illnesses, lower desires, or other challenges, so that he can help remove them from your heart. If you keep them inside, they will grow, and you will fail the test. But if you confess them to him, he will guide you on a path to purify yourself from them. If you have a sin, don't let it fester within you—reveal it to your Shaykh. If you have a desire that has taken control of your heart, don't keep it hidden—speak about it. This is how Allāh will reform you through the hands of your Shaykh.

As for those who pretend to be saints, displaying piety and faith while their hearts are filled with filth, Allāh will expose them when they enter His path. Always wayfare with humility and do not give importance to your ego. Do not hide anything from your Shaykh, whether in worldly matters or matters of faith. If you wish to take a job, seek your Shaykh's permission. If you wish to marry, consult your Shaykh, and if you wish to travel, turn to him. Do not proceed with anything without his approval, so you don't later regret what your ego has chosen for you. Any action performed without your Shaykh's guidance and permission is cut off, for he is the source of abundance (*kawthar*), and whoever opposes him is the one who is truly cut off (*mabtūr*).

Draw from his abundance in every movement and stillness (*sukūn*), and do not undertake anything without his permission, blessings, and prayers. Every permission you receive from him is connected to Allāh, and through it, along with the action that accompanies it, you will reach the knowledge of Allāh by the blessings of your Shaykh. Any action taken without his permission or connection creates a separation (*faṣl*) between you and Allāh, leading you down. It is a path among the paths of devils that distances you from Him.

Remember, the ten companions promised Paradise were always in the company of our master, the Messenger of Allāh ﷺ and they sought his guidance in every matter. This is why they attained such a prestigious rank.

Know that anything that cuts you off from your Shaykh or places a barrier between you and him is a rebellious devil, for the Shaykh has not placed any barrier between himself and any disciple. On the contrary, he has opened his door to all. This is a grace from Allāh, granted only to those He has chosen.

C. Fear of the Elevated Station

This does not mean that your Shaykh is like other people. When you sit with him, know that you are sitting with the Image of the Most Merciful, the Vicegerent of the Almighty, and the Inheritor of the Prophet ﷺ. Do not be deceived by his outward appearance, for by Allāh, if his light were to fully manifest, it would obliterate our very essence. Sit with him with the sole intention of receiving from his knowledge and blessings, and avoid staring at his face for too long or engaging in casual conversation.

Always be cautious of yourself and guard against crossing any boundaries with your Shaykh, for he is a pure mirror. If he loves you, the Prophet ﷺ will love you, and so will Allāh. If he dislikes you, the Prophet ﷺ will dislike you, and so will Allāh. Honor him with the respect due to him by Allāh, as it is mentioned in the *ḥadīth qudsī* (sacred *ḥadīth*): "Whoever shows enmity to a *walī*, I declare war upon him."

Consider his words as a divine revelation, even if spoken in jest, for a *walī* does not jest in the way ordinary people do; all his words are truth. Be mindful of every warning he gives, even if it is wrapped in humor, and rejoice in every glad tiding he offers, even if it seems playful, for when he speaks, his words manifest in the universe. So, both fear and rejoice at the same time.

Do not flatter your Shaykh with phrases like "I love you, Shaykh," or other expressions whose true weight you do not yet understand. Such words will lead you into deep spiritual trials and place you in a test for which you are unprepared, as you claim knowledge you do not possess. Know that the Shaykh does not appreciate flattery because he perceives the hidden realities of the soul. Be yourself, and do not pretend to be something you are not. In this way, Allāh will have mercy on you, for the Shaykh loves those who are truthful and dislikes those who are hypocritical and deceptive. Those who are honest with the Shaykh and do not pretend to be what they are not will find the Shaykh guiding them on the journey with beauty (*jamāl*). In contrast, those who deceive and fabricate will face the sternness of the path and the intensity of spiritual rigor.

D. The Jealousy of the Saint

Know—God, His Messenger, and His Saint know best—that Allāh is The Mighty; He destroys anyone who challenges Him in any attribute or competes with Him in any matter. He is The One, The Supreme, The Owner of the physical Kingdom, The Possessor of Majesty and Beauty. Everything apart from Him is but an illusion, devoid of true reality; destined for nothingness and inevitable annihilation. Yet, He, the Exalted, loved the Beloved—peace and blessings be upon him—drew him near, and made him a manifestation for both the whole and the part, by the secret of His saying, **Allāh is the *Walī*.**

There is no gateway to Him except through the name *al-Walī*, which was manifested in the physical world through His righteous servant and in the spiritual realms through the successful Chosen One ﷺ. Thus, the saint is the secret of both non-existence and existence, the connector and separator between nothingness and eternity. Through this gateway, God has granted him a share in all names and attributes, and realized him in the depths of the Divine Essence.

Thus, the secret of **Allāh is the Light of the heavens and the earth** was revealed through him. And He has made this secret accessible to the people of the earth through the secret of **Allāh is the *Walī* of those who believe, bringing them out of the darknesses into light.**[18]

If the Most Merciful bestows upon you the Pledge of al-Riḍwān, and the Beneficent nourishes you with the light of the Chosen One from the fountain of tranquility through the hand of the righteous *walī*, then in his presence, do not mention other *awliyā'* or righteous individuals outside the clear chain of transmission. Otherwise, you would be like a dog biting the hand of its master, who feeds and quenches its thirst from the *Kawthar* of the Most Just. It would be as if those previous righteous ones—may Allāh be pleased with them—were the ones who granted you this ultimate blessing. When the Cherished one (the Shaykh) honors you, show gratitude by turning solely to him, not to others. If you show reverence to someone else in what he has honored you with, he has the right to take it back so that you may learn proper etiquette before the one who has favored you, lest you diminish His favor by neglecting his grace.

. . . .

18 *Sūra* 2. *Al-Baqarah,* verse 257.

Establish your *qibla* from the beginning, and be dignified through His dignity, beloved through His love, and annihilated in His presence. See no favor except as coming to you through His affection, and no merit except as attained by His power. It is He who brought you out of your death among the shadows, by the evidence and the proof, by the Sunnah and the Qur'ān—whether you accept or resist this fact, embrace or oppose this truth. Be like the angels of the Most Merciful, prostrating to the Vicegerent (*khalīfa*) of the Most Merciful, submitting to the secret of Vicegerency, which He has made a barrier for you against death in the realm of oblivion.

Do not display your library, which has merely pacified your heart, as if you had already traversed the path before him. We were like dust on the shelves of oblivion, mindlessly chewing on pages like beasts, devoid of flavor or true life. Our silence in refraining from speaking of what we do not truly possess is a virtue, and forgetting the lines we have stored from others is a path to true attainment. Empty yourself of what you have read about the lives of the righteous, so you do not fall into the delusion that you are among them. You and I are nothing but a bundle of sins, crawling on all fours toward the harbor of peace, solely by the grace of the One who grants it. Always remember that poverty is the secret to true wealth and that light only reveals itself in the midst of darkness.

Empty yourself of all that came to you before, for it is a barrier, and do not return to it unless the *walī* himself guides you back. You will not truly enter the path until you have—at the very least—let go of the illusions you held before reaching the *walī*. Place everything and everyone you valued before entering the exalted gate on the scales that do not deceive: did it lead you from darkness to light, and did it realize you in the station of awakened vision (*mushāhada*), or did it keep you in the illusion of falsehood? From this, you will know that anyone you encountered before, who claimed to guide you on this path, deceiving you with false pretenses, is nothing more than a fraud. Forget him, empty yourself of him, so that your breath may draw closer to the Breath of the Most Merciful (*nafas ar-raḥmān*).

Remember that Allāh says in the Qur'ān, **Allāh is the Walī**[19], not "Allāh is the *Awliyā'*" (plural). He also says, **And those who disbelieve, their *awliyā'* are the despots (*ṭāghūt*).**[20] Thus, the true *walī* is singular, and anyone else who claims it falsely is a pretender and an accomplice of the *ṭāghūt*. As there is no true

....

19 *Ibid.*
20 *Ibid.*

Shaykh except the one who reveals the inner secret; and remember that even the Arabs of *jāhiliyya* were well aware of the futility of empty words.

What we have explained here—by the grace of Allāh and His *walī*—is the greatest treasure of guidance. Whoever does not grasp it halts his journey, and whoever realizes it tastes the sweetness of its nectar. So, O Allāh, make us like bees that drink from this chosen blessing by the grace of the Master of the *awliyā'*.

IV.

Dynamism in the Path of Allāh

A. Testifying as an Individual Obligation for the Witness

Know—and Allāh, His Messenger, and His *walī* know best—that movement is the secret of stillness, and stillness is the secret of movement. Allāh, the Almighty, loved the prophets, messengers, and saints for what they manifested in the universe through their movement, allowing the knowledge of Allāh to be revealed. Had they suppressed the divine favor bestowed upon them, people would have remained in ignorance. Allāh, the Almighty, says:

O Messenger, convey what has been revealed to you from your Lord. If you do not, then you have not conveyed His message. And Allāh will protect you from the people. Indeed, Allāh does not guide the disbelieving people.[21]

. . . .

21 *Sūra 5. Al-Māʾidah*, verse 67.

Whoever does not convey the messages of Allāh does not protect himself from the harm of people. The disciple's will is not complete without sharing what Allāh has revealed to him through the blessings of his Shaykh, specifically by testifying to the light originating from the Lote Tree of the Furthest Boundary (*sidrat al-muntahā*). Whoever stubbornly withholds this light departs from the protection from harm, as decreed by the noble verse, and opens the door wide to enemies. Such a person either denies and discards the goodness bestowed upon him by the Shaykh, and these are the most despicable and cursed of seekers, for they see the light and its bearer—may his secret be sanctified—as a source of shame. The second type of misguided individuals who fail to convey this grace are those who believe themselves superior to this blessing or its bearer—may his noble secret be sanctified—and these are the most deluded and insignificant of the blind.

Whoever conveys the message of Allāh's light secures protection for himself from all harms, both great and small, and is drawn closer by the inheritor of the Infallible into the presence of the Absolute. He is loved with the love of the Chosen One ﷺ, his understanding is revived, and his path is guided toward true spiritual richness.

The first and least form of this conveyance is to testify to Allāh's grace and the blessing of His *walī*, recognizing that it brought him out of blindness and guided him onto the path of the Eternal.

Whoever does not bear this testimony is cut off from divine knowledge, shackled by the chains of illusion (the sensory realm), and cannot escape it. Whoever does not return the favor to its rightful owner is lost and deserves nothing but the stick.

So, O Allāh, make it easy for us to convey Your messages, and grant us unwavering determination from the wellspring of Your sanctified, saintly power.

Resist your *nafs* (lower self), which seeks to prevent you from reaping the fruits of righteous action through laziness and fear—fear of people, rather than fear of the Lord of all people. Strive against it, for it will try to hold you back from engaging in the noblest of deeds: proclaiming His greatest blessing, His exalted light.

And know—and Allāh knows best—that Mawlānā Shaykh—may his noble secret be sanctified—once told us that whoever bears true witness to the light of Allāh and presents himself to proclaim this unparalleled blessing to the world, Allāh will remove from him three veils of darkness, his Shaykh will grant him knowledge of the heart, and the Chosen One ﷺ will testify that he is among the people of safety on the Day of Judgment. As for those who do not, a banner of treason will be raised over them, and they will be muzzled with the fire of humiliation on that Day.

B. Continue to Call to the Path of Allāh Until Mercies Are Renewed Within You

Know—and Allāh and His *walī* know best—that the highest form of striving (*jihād*) in the path of Allāh is to make it known, and the shortest path to the heart of sainthood is to speak of the blessing of the divine light. Every act of worship you perform—whether fasting or prayer—benefits only yourself, but spreading the path and making it known benefits everyone. As the Messenger of Allāh said to the *walī* of Allāh, Sayyidunā ʿAlī—peace be upon them: "By Allāh! If a single person is guided by Allāh through you, it will be better for you than [acquiring] red camels."[22] If this applies to guiding someone to the station of Islam, how much greater is the reward for guiding creation to the light of faith, as our Shaykh—may Allāh sanctify his secret—has said?

Know that laziness, fear of others, and pretending to observe *ādāb* can prevent a disciple from convey-

....

22　Al-Bukhārī, *Ṣaḥīḥ al-Bukhārī, Kitāb al-Maghāzī* (*The Book of Military Expeditions*), ḥadīth 3009 (*Book 56, ḥadīth* 154).

ing the divine messages that the Shaykh—may Allāh sanctify his secret—has entrusted to him. Many who have become stagnant on their spiritual journey have done so by following these misguided paths, eventually passing away without ever truly experiencing the Breath of the Most Merciful. The path to Allāh is a sacred message—the locus of its *sukūn* (stillness) lies in the *jabarūt* (the realm of God's absolute being) of sainthood, its creativity in the *malakūt* (spiritual or angelic realm) of prophecy, and its movement in what you manifest through the guidance of your Shaykh in the *mulk* (physical realm).

Whoever advances on the path of Allāh with the intention of making it known and becoming a cause for its flourishing is elevated by the Almighty and chosen. Allāh bends his surroundings—both people and circumstances—to his favor, making him a leader among his peers, with his words respected and his banner held high. Conversely, the opposite is also true.

The Shaykh—may Allāh sanctify his secret—does not incline his heart toward those who are miserly and reluctant in their efforts of *da'wa*, nor does he draw them near, even if they mistakenly believe they are close in a physical sense. But the one who makes the path to Allāh the foremost of all causes and concerns, the secret behind all blessings, and dedicates his efforts to spreading the message and defending the divine light, is loved by the Shaykh, drawn close in the Highest Assembly (*al-mala' al-a'lā*), and blessed in both the higher and lower realms. The true disciple is the one who manifests the divine trust placed in him, standing firm against his critics, thereby earning the honor of following the path and erasing hypocrisy from his being.

This station is higher than mere testimony, for its essence is continuously renewed within the depths of sainthood, and its connection is fortified with the secret of divine care. The treasures of the righteous *walī* are spiritual, and whoever dedicates themselves to calling others to Allāh's path engages, even from afar, with the spirit of the Vicegerent, the *walī*. In doing so, he pours out the matured mercies he has reaped from his connection with the Shaykh to the servants of the Lord of creation. Thereafter, his Shaykh—may Allāh sanctify his secret—renews these mercies within his heart and broadens the sphere of his understanding of the subtle divine signs.

But as for the one who suppresses the light within himself, his horizon will not expand, and his understanding of the divine secret will not mature. He is like a fruit-laden tree whose fruits are not harvested; such a tree will not continue to bear fruit in the years to come. However, the tree whose fruits are harvested benefits others and becomes even more fruitful in the subsequent years.

Know that sainthood is tied to patience in acts of obedience and consistently seeking proximity to the Lord of creation. The Messenger of Allāh, peace be upon him, said: "The most beloved of deeds to Allāh are those done consistently, even if they are few."[23] And the Lord of Majesty said through the tongue of the Chosen One, peace be upon him: "My servant continues to draw near to Me with voluntary acts of worship until I love him."[24]

Thus, the key to fruitful *da'wa* lies in consistency and disciplining the *nafs* to maintain it. Dedicate a specific time each day or week to inviting others to the path of Allāh and manifesting it with the blessings of understanding and creativity that the *walī* of Allāh has granted you. Remember that al-Ṣiddīq (Abū Bakr) and al-Fārūq ('Umar)—may Allāh be pleased with them both—used to compete in spreading the Ahmadian messages, and for this reason, they were the closest, after Allāh and His *walī*, to the heart of the Messenger, peace be upon him.

Know that if you journey on this path, you become an isthmus (*barzakh*) among the Shaykh's isthmuses,

....

23 Al-Bukhārī, *Ṣaḥīḥ al-Bukhārī, Kitāb al-Īmān* (*The Book of Faith*), *ḥadīth* 6464 (*Book 81, ḥadīth 53*

24 Al-Bukhārī, *Ṣaḥīḥ al-Bukhārī, Kitāb al-Riqāq* (*The Book of Softening the Hearts*), *ḥadīth* 6502 (*Book 81, ḥadīth 38*).

reaping the divine bounties of both worlds, the seen and the unseen, outwardly and inwardly. By maintaining these acts of obedience, you board the train of divine pleasure; but if you abandon them, you descend into the station of denial. So, O Allāh, make us among those who persist in performing the voluntary acts of preaching *maʿrifa*.

As the *walī* of Allāh, Sīdī Aḥmad Al-ʾAlāwī—may Allāh be pleased with him—said: "Strive, and you will witness the sweetest benefits."

C. Speak to the Common People According to Their Level of Understanding

The Prophet ﷺ said: "We have been commanded to address people according to their level of understanding."[25]

Mawlānā ʿAlī—peace be upon him—said: "Speak to people only according to their level of knowledge. Would you want Allāh and His Messenger to be considered liars?"[26]

....

25 Al-Sulamī, *Tafsīr*, chapter 1, page 377; al-Ghazālī, *Iḥyāʾ ʿUlūm al-Dīn*, chapter 1, page 144; Ibn ʿArabī, *al-Futūḥāt al-Makkiyya*, chapter 2, page 549; al-Shaʿrānī, *Al-Ṭabaqāt al-Kubrā*, chapter 1, page 21; *Jawāhir al-Maʿānī*, chapter 2, page 211

26 Al-Bukhārī, *Ṣaḥīḥ al-Bukhārī*, *Kitāb al-ʿIlm* (*Book of Knowledge*), Bāb 1, *ḥadīth* 127.

Sayyidunā Ibn Masʿūd—may Allāh be pleased with him—said: "If you speak to a people about matters beyond their understanding, it will only cause corruption among some of them."[27]

Had our Shaykh—may Allāh sanctify his secret—not followed this principle, none of us, being essentially deniers, would have followed him. Anyone who thinks otherwise is merely displaying arrogance, for the *walī*—may Allāh sanctify his secret—due to his deep immersion in the ocean of divine realities and his comprehensive grasp of both esoteric and exoteric sciences, can only be truly understood by his Lord. Do not assume that the drops of truth he has shown us from the oceans of his knowledge give us the right to rebuke those outside the circle of *wilāya* for the presumptions they hold from their speculative knowledge. We are insignificant, standing in the same station in the eyes of the Shaykh—may Allāh sanctify his secret—and were it not for his kindness and gentleness with us, we would have fled like prey from a predator.

Our gentleness in dealing with the ideas expressed by our brothers who are still outside the circle of light is, in itself, a form of daʿwa and a reflection of the Shaykh's gentleness flowing through us, who are cer-

....

27 *Al-ʿAynī, ʿUmdat al-Qarī Sharḥ Ṣaḥīḥ al-Bukhārī,* Vol. 2, p. 308.

tainly deniers. We employ this gentleness in inviting them until Allāh takes their hands and leads them to the shore of realities—that is, Mawlānā al-Walī—may Allāh sanctify his secret.

On the contrary, harshness leads only to destruction, discord, evil, and repulsion. The Messenger of Allāh, peace be upon him, said: "Whoever believes in Allāh and the Last Day, let him speak good or remain silent."[28] Thus, silence becomes a confirmed Sunna (*sunna muʾakkada*) when we are unable to discern the source of understanding of those distant from the truths who oppose us. We find ourselves in the same position—or even worse—when we place our limited understanding against the boundless wisdom of our Shaykh—may Allāh sanctify his secret.

Allāh Almighty says: **So by mercy from Allāh, [O Muḥammad], you were gentle with them. Had you been harsh and hard-hearted, they would have dispersed from around you. So pardon them, ask forgiveness for them, and consult them in the matter.**[29]

And Allāh, His Messenger, and His *walī* know best.

....

28 Al-Bukhārī, *Ṣaḥīḥ al-Bukhārī, Kitāb al-Adāb (The Book of Manners)*, ḥadīth No. 6475.
29 *Sūra* 3. *Āl-ʿImrān*, verse 159.

D. Return the Blessing to the Shaykh

Know—and Allāh, His Messenger, and His *walī* know best—that everything Allāh manifests on your tongue when calling others to Him, any divine understanding of the words of Allāh and His Messenger, or any physical miracle, has its source in the *walī* of Allāh, not in yourself or your darkened *nafs*.

Therefore, do not attribute the blessings that Allāh has bestowed upon you to yourself, nor think that you are the origin of these blessings. You and I are darkness upon darkness, and if it were not for the spirit of the Shaykh—may Allāh sanctify his secret—blowing into us the breath of the Most Merciful, we would have remained in that darkness for eternity. Allāh, the Exalted, says: **And is one who was dead and We gave him life and made for him a light by which to walk among the people like one who is in darkness, never to emerge from it?**[30]

Our Lord says, "**We made**," not "I made," thereby associating the *walī* in the realm of contingencies in the origin of the grace descending from his spirit in the realm of power. Therefore, do not involve yourself in the sphere of power or in its causes, for you and I are nothing more than letters written by the *walī* with the power of Allāh in the hidden divine record. We

....

30 *Sūra 6. Al-Anʿām*, verse 122.

have no power or strength except through them, and our duty is to observe proper etiquette toward them in the world of contingencies, and to praise and thank Allāh for guiding us to this. Verily, we would not have been guided if Allāh had not guided us.

Indeed, Allāh, the Exalted, has granted the *walī* powers that surpass human comprehension and defy description. These powers include the keys to managing the world and exercising authority over both the particulars and the universals. Our Lord, the Exalted, declares through the tongue of the Messenger of Allah, peace be upon him: "Whoever shows enmity to a friend of Mine, I have declared war against him."[31] This signifies that the *walī* is a distributor of success and happiness, as well as a source of worry and misery, according to the explicit wording of the *ḥadīth qudsī*. He is an intermediary between these states, influencing them without being influenced by their separation or connection.

The Messenger of Allah, peace be upon him, also said: "I am the *sayyid* (master) of the children of Adam, and I do not boast." Additionally, he remarked

. . . .

31 Al-Bukhārī, Ṣaḥīḥ al-Bukhārī, (*Book of Softening the Hearts*), Chapter on Humility, *ḥadīth* No. 6502

about Sayyidunā al-Ḥasan, peace be upon them both: "This son of mine is a *sayyid* (master)."[32]

Thus, *siyāda* (mastery) is an intrinsic aspect of *wilāya* (sainthood) due to its inherited nature, as indicated in the aforementioned *hadīth* of our master, the Messenger of Allah, peace be upon him. When we reflect on the word *sayyid* (master), it can be broken down into S/*yad*, or say the «secret of the hand» (*sirr al-yadd*). The *walī* is the hand through which one pledges allegiance to Allah in order to attain self-knowledge, as stated in the verse: **The Hand of Allah is over their hands.** Beyond that, they embody the secret of this hand, executing divine decrees in accordance with Allah's will. As Allah says, **Whoever breaks his oath only breaks it to the detriment of himself; and whoever fulfills what he has covenanted with Allah, He will grant him a great reward.**[33]

. . . .

32 Al-Nasā'ī, *Ṣaḥīḥ al-Nasā'ī*, "Kitāb al-Zakāh" (*The Book of Charity*), *hadīth* No. 1409. Al-Bukhārī, *Ṣaḥīḥ al-Bukhārī*, "Kitāb al-Hibah" (*The Book of Gifts*), *hadīth* No. 2704. Abū Dāwūd, *Sunan Abī Dāwūd*, "Kitāb al-Adab" (*The Book of Manners*), *hadīth* No. 4662. Al-Tirmidhī, *Sunan al-Tirmidhī*, "Kitāb al-Zuhd" (*The Book of Asceticism*), *hadīth* No. 3773. Al-Nasā'ī, *Ṣaḥīḥ al-Nasā'ī*, "Kitāb al-Zakāh" (*The Book of Charity*), *hadīth* No. 1410 (same wording). Aḥmad ibn Ḥanbal, *Musnad Aḥmad*, "Musnad al-Makkiyyīn" (*The Musnad of the Makkans*), *hadīth* No. 20392.

33 *Sūra* 48, *Al-Fatḥ*, verse 10

Do not let your mind, O reader, consider this impossible, for it is clearly stated regarding Mawlānā Al-Khidr, peace be upon him, in the Holy Qur'ān, where my Lord, your Lord, and the Lord of all things says: **He said, 'If you follow me, do not ask me about anything until I reveal its truth to you.'**[34]

God did not merely state that He would make something happen—this is beyond question. Instead, He said: "Until I reveal its truth (*uḥditha dhikrā*) to you," indicating that it is the *walī* who brings down revelation into the realm of contingencies, a matter that has even perplexed prophets and messengers, peace be upon them.

And if you doubt our words, continue reading the rest of the noble *Sūra* to witness how the *walī*, through the secret of the Hand of Divine capacity and power (*qudra*), acts within the cosmos. He is the mover in both the realm of contingencies (the Hand) and the realm of decrees (the Secret), by virtue of his *siyāda*, through his inheritance of the Prophetic choiceness (*iṣṭifā'*) from the source of choiceness.

This is why, in earlier times, people were marked by submission and serenity: they never dared challenge the *wilāya* (sainthood) or those illuminated by its light, fearing that the Hand of *qudra* might act

....

34 *Sūra* 18. *Al-Kahf*, verse 70

unfavorably in the realm of causes. Yet, the wretched have always existed, especially in our time, where the virtues of submission have been lost, and every pretender claims the right to interpret texts, dismiss mediation (*wāsiṭa*), elevate ignorance, and accuse others of innovation.

It is narrated about our Shaykh and master, the knower of God, Mawlānā al-ʿArabī al-Darqāwī, may Allah sanctify his secret, that he was once in the market after shaving his head. A foolish man approached him, seized his head in front of the crowd, and mockingly repeatedly said, "What kind of melon is this?" Not long after, a mule in the market trampled over the man's head, leading to his death. When people came to ask the *walī* of God, Mawlānā al-ʿArabī al-Darqāwī, about what had happened, he replied: "I did nothing to him; it was the Owner of the melon who became jealous of His melon."

The Master of the Hand moved the secret (*sirr*), distributing misfortune (*shaqāʾ*) and bringing forth the event, manipulating the threads of causes while adorning himself with the veil of concealment, as the people of that time surrendered to him the reality of *siyāda*. And if these words do not convince you, then recall what God said in the *ḥadīth* about the righteous *walī,* whose every movement, stillness, attribute, and essence are from God; his supplications are answered, and he is a shield and refuge from every evil, both on land and sea.

As for the heedless disciple, to whom God has granted ease in life through the hand of *wilāya*—**And made me blessed wherever I may be**[35]—and who attributes the blessings he perceives to himself and his own actions, while harboring ill thoughts toward the Master of Masters, he is more heedless than the common people who oppose the *walī*. Those people have not witnessed his miracles firsthand, whereas this disciple has seen them through clear evidence and proof. Let not his patience with our lack of gratitude deceive us, for by God, if he wished to ignite the flames of contraction (*qabḍ*) in anyone's life, the decrees would weave causes for him such that death would be more desirable than life.

Do you really believe that the fate of a ship cutting through the sea to reach the shore of safety is under the captain's control? This is a delusion created by the minds of both the captain and ourselves, born from the habitual practice that the Hand of *qudra* has ordained for such matters. The reality is that if the sea wished to destroy the ship and its captain, it would surge and drown the illusions of his control over the

....

35 *Sūra 17. Maryam*, verse 31

helm. Apply this analogy to the *walī*, for he is the Sea of Reality and *sharīʿa*, the secret of the Hand behind every movement and stillness.

As we have said, by the blessings of the Master of the Time—may Allāh sanctify his secret:

The Ship and the Sea

O heart, wearied by the burdens of the "I,"
Submerged in the depths of estrangement
and the trials of vain inclinations,
You gain nothing but endless toil if
you perceive your earthly being as heaven.

You are a ship upon a self-sufficient Sea,
Adrift among all that perceives you as an "I."

Though unaware, you remain captive to the Sea;
For if the Sea surges, it drowns all your hopes.

Yet, if the Sea desires your prosperity,
It fashions the waves to become your allies,
Moving all creation for you, to the harbor
of safety, the port of aspirations.

Seek, then, the path of softness and ease,
And remember you are from a despised water.

Fear your own self and every "I,"
For your control lies only over illusions.

Implore the Sea with every "I,"
Knowing it is not truly you who implores.

As the push of the waves is your
sole fuel in the way of salvation,
But if the Sea wills, those same
waves will drown you.

Do not imagine that you have any right over God or that the abundance you live in comes from your own doing. It might be a trap or a path laid by Satan, crafted by the illusion of your control over contingencies. Do not be deceived by the apparent weakness shown by the *walī*, for he is the secret behind destiny and the one who has bestowed every expansion (*bast*) and beauty (*jamāl*) upon you. By God, I swear thrice, if you belittle him and fail to uphold the *ādāb* with him, and the walī wills you to fall, the gates of the earth and heavens will close upon you for what you might perceive as the slightest of reasons. The fires of affliction will burn within you, time will turn against you, and the circles of fate will tighten around you...

Fear your own self and do not attribute any good to it. Instead, ascribe it to your Shaykh, the master of the time, blessed in every moment as confirmed by the Qur'ān. Arm yourself with supplication when calamity befalls you, and do not cease seeking intercession through him. Do not claim what does not belong to you or me from the lofty ranks of spiritual knowledge, for this path is the path of true men. As for someone like you and me, we have only words, while the spiritual will (*himma*) comes from him, not from us. Only those whom God has intended well in this lower realm understand this discourse, and God, His Messenger, and His walī know the truth.

O God, be gentle with us, lift every hardship from us, and never test us, O Lord, by the honor of him through whom You have distributed happiness and misery, and by the honor of the prayers and peace upon his grandfather, Abū al-Qāsim, the flower of all creation.

E. "Woe to Those Who Say What They Do not Do"

Know—and Allāh knows best—that speaking is the characteristic of the hypocrites: **On that Day, the hypocrites, men and women, will say...**[36] While action is the characteristic of the believers: **And say, 'Do [righteous deeds]; for Allāh will see your deeds, and [so will] His Messenger and the believers. And**

....

36   *Sūra 57. Al Ḥadīd,* verse 13.

you will be returned to the Knower of the unseen and the witnessed, and He will inform you of what you used to do.'[37]

Do not corrupt your faith with careless words, and do not hasten to your Shaykh with a momentary thought, claiming that you will perform a certain deed for the sake of Allah's path. The Shaykh—may Allāh sanctify his secret—does not forget and will hold you accountable for your words, either rewarding you with the gardens of fulfillment or leaving you to face the disgrace of abandoning them. It is wiser, if a beneficial thought for the path crosses your mind, to contemplate it thoroughly, study its foundations for success seriously, and prepare the means for its implementation. Then, seek permission either to share it or to commence it. Know that the *walī* often guides you toward matters that align with your service to the path and its promotion. So, follow what he outlines for you, arm yourself with diligence, and guard your tongue from speaking without action.

F. There is no Path without Adherence, and no Adherence without *Sharīʿa*

Know—and Allāh, His Messenger, and His walī know best—that this path, which the Prophet, peace

....

37 *Sūra* 9. At-Tawba, verse 105.

be upon him, delineated with his own hand, can only be followed through adherence, and it cannot be borne by any innovator. Whoever desires to reach the destination must follow the elite of the progeny of the Messenger—peace be upon him and his family—and true adherence can only be achieved by seeking the gate of *sharīʿa* and exalting its rituals.

Exalting the symbols of religion is an exaltation of the one who manifested them, the praised one—peace be upon him. Allāh, the Exalted, says: **And whoever honors the symbols of Allah—indeed, it is from the piety of hearts.**[38]

Exalting the symbols of religion is a sign of piety in the heart and a mark of divine care for the one in whom this virtue has settled. The one who sees special value in the manifestations of religion and the Sunna, who strives to follow them and whose heart is grieved by their neglect or imperfection, is the one whom Allāh has endowed with the grace of annihilation in the blessed Muḥammadan form. This form is represented in your Shaykh in your era, drawing from the source that gathers all times—our master, the Messenger, peace be upon him. This is the purest form brought forth for humanity and the highest standard by which all things are measured.

....

38 *Sūra 22. Al Ḥajj*, verse 32.

This image (*ṣūra*) is attributed to its inheritor in every era, and it is the image of our Shaykh—may Allāh sanctify his secret—in this era.

Know, therefore, that the Prophetic form is the source of all religious manifestations—be they speech, actions, or approvals. If these manifestations have reached us through authentic chains of transmission as preserved by the scholars—may Allāh protect them—then they are truly alive in our Shaykh—may Allāh sanctify his secret. Do not be like those about whom Allāh says: **And you see them looking at you, but they do not see,**[39] meaning they observe the trace of the heavens in the lower realm—peace be upon him—yet they remain heedless of its essence. They fail to recognize in his movements, actions, approvals, and form the messages emanating from the heart of the divine lamp. Instead, they attribute his apparent perfection, peace be upon him, to the lowest realm due to their foolishness and baseness.

Do not be like those about whom Allāh says: "And they say, 'What is [with] this Messenger that he eats food and walks in the markets?'"[40] This means do not be like those who perceive the Messenger, peace be upon him, through their stomachs, becoming slaves

....

39 *Sūra 7. Al-A'rāf*, verse 198.
40 *Sūra 25. Al Furqān*, verse 7.

to gluttony and commerce, and turning away from the worship of the Real: "They have forgotten Allāh, so He has made them forget their selves,"[41] and thus they walk on their bellies.

Had they been among the people of exaltation and ascension, they would have seen in his eating and walking in the markets a path to ascend to the Lord of food and markets. They would have extracted the essence and nectar to fill the vessel of faith with the light of the Lord of the worlds.

It is narrated that 'Abd Allāh ibn 'Umar—may Allāh be pleased with him—would not eat until he brought a poor person to eat with him. Nāfi' said: "I brought a man to eat with him, and he ate a lot. Ibn 'Umar said, 'O Nāfi', do not bring this man to me again. I heard the Prophet say, 'The believer eats in one intestine, while the disbeliever eats in seven intestines.'" 'Amr said: "Abū Nahīk was a gluttonous man. Ibn 'Umar said to him, 'The Prophet, peace be upon him, said, 'The disbeliever eats in seven intestines.' Abū Nahīk responded, 'I believe in Allāh and His Messenger.'"[42]

....

41 *Sūra 59. Al-Hashr,* verse 19.
42 Al-Bukhārī, *Ṣaḥīḥ al-Bukhārī, Kitāb al-Aṭ'imah* (*The Book of Foods*), *ḥadīth* No. 5393.

This means that when the Prophet, peace be upon him, accompanied him in eating, he found a way to attain realization in the station of faith in Allāh and His message, allowing him to distinguish between the people of faith and piety and those of disbelief and deviation—between the blessed and the distant. His compass was adjusted—may Allāh be pleased with him—his path straightened, and his inner light was illuminated by contemplating the Prophet's judgment in a simple act of life: eating. The Prophet, peace be upon him, said: "Do not befriend anyone except a believer, and let no one eat your food except the pious."[43]

Thus, those who are negligent in following the Sunna of the Prophet, peace be upon him, who lean towards imitating disbelievers in dress, food, and social interactions, and who are embarrassed by the Sunna and view it as backwardness, are akin to those who could not see in his noble appearance a path to Allāh. Their lower selves dominated them, diverting them from immersion in the light of the Real and leading them astray. Allāh the Exalted says: **They follow nothing but assumption and what [their]**

....

43 Al-Tirmidhī, *Sunan al-Tirmidhī*, *Kitāb al-Zuhd* (*The Book of Asceticism*), ḥadīth No. 2395.

souls desire, while guidance has already come to them from their Lord.[44]

Allāh also says: **Have you seen the one who takes as his god his own desire? Then Allāh has left him astray due to knowledge and has set a seal upon his hearing and his heart and placed over his vision a veil. So who will guide him after Allāh? Will you not then remember?**[45] Whenever you deviate from the example of the chosen one, peace be upon him, you are sealed off, as stated in the verse. O Allāh, grant us safety, grant us safety!

It is narrated from Ibn 'Umar—may Allāh be pleased with him—that the Messenger of Allāh, peace be upon him, said: "Whoever imitates a people is one of them."[46]

It is narrated from 'Abd Allāh ibn 'Amr ibn al-'Āṣ—may Allāh be pleased with them—that the Messenger of Allah, peace be upon him, saw me wearing two dyed garments and said: "These are garments of disbelievers, so do not wear them."[47] The Prophet, peace be upon him, thus clarified that the prohibition

. . . .

44 *Sūra 53. An-Najm,* verse 23.

45 *Sūra 45. Al-Jāthiya,* verse 23

46 Abū Dāwūd, *Sunan Abī Dāwūd, Kitāb al-Libās* (*The Book of Clothing*), *ḥadīth* No. 4031.

47 Muslim, *Ṣaḥīḥ Muslim, Kitāb al-Libās wa'l-Zīnah* (*The Book of Clothing and Adornment*), *ḥadīth* No. 2077.

of wearing such garments was due to their association with the disbelievers.

It is also narrated from Ibn 'Umar—may Allāh be pleased with them—that the Messenger of Allah, peace be upon him, said: "Oppose the polytheists: trim the mustaches and let the beards grow."[48]

Thus, the folk of God throughout the ages have greatly revered the Sunnah of the Prophet, peace be upon him, beginning with its outward manifestations, and none of them have ever been lenient in following it. Among them were those who even refrained from taking any concessions. Sayyidunā Abū Bakr al-Ṣiddīq —may Allāh be pleased with him—said: "I will not leave anything the Messenger of Allah used to do except that I will do it. I fear that if I leave anything from his practices, I will go astray."[49]

'Umar ibn 'Abd al-'Azīz—may Allāh have mercy on him—said: "No one has the right to hold an opinion when there is a sunna established by the Messenger of Allah."[50]

....

48 Al-Bukhārī, *Ṣaḥīḥ al-Bukhārī*, *Kitāb al-Libās* (*The Book of Clothing*), ḥadīth No. 5892.

49 Muḥammad ibn Sa'd, *Ṭabaqāt al-Kubrā*, *Dhikr Abī Bakr al-Ṣiddīq* (*The Mention of Abū Bakr al-Ṣiddīq*), Vol. 3, p. 140.

50 Ibn 'Abd al-Barr, *Jāmi' Bayān al-'Ilm wa Faḍlihi*, *Bāb Fī Faḍl al-'Ilm wal-'Ulamā'* (*The Chapter on the Virtue of Knowledge and Scholars*), Vol. 2, p. 33.

Let no one blame but himself if he neglects the gate of *sharīʿa* and uses leniency as an excuse. The Shaykh—may Allāh sanctify his secret—is a mercy written by Allāh for the pious, but for the wicked, there is the fire of Hell in this world before the Hereafter. How many seekers have lived in misery due to their negligence in fulfilling obligations and not upholding the covenant of Allāh; their sorrows are endless, and their prayers go unanswered. Conversely, how many devout, reverent followers, fearful of Allāh's boundaries and fulfilling His covenant, drink from His bounties, served by the worlds, and upon them descend the subtleties of mercy and the sciences of divine knowledge at all times.

Do not neglect any obligation except that you fulfill it fully, and do not leave any disliked matter except that you abandon it completely. Fear playing with the rituals established by Allāh and daring to cross His boundaries, for the one who has been granted the gate of certainty has a reckoning more severe than those with only the report of certainty. Remember that your Shaykh loves only those whom Allāh loves, and Allāh loves only those who add the supererogatory to the obligatory, whose being has settled on the reality of *īmān* after *islām*.

Know that half of the worries and sorrows of the seeker on the path to Allāh stem from neglecting the rights of Allāh, and the other half from not recognizing this inner disease. So, O Allāh, make us among those who follow the illiterate Prophet in every small and large matter, until our form is annihilated in the nobility of his form, and his beauty manifests within us as it did in Mawlānā Shaykh—may Allāh sanctify his secret—even if it be just a speck, so that we may become like a hair in his absolute beauty.

V.

Spending on the Path of Allāh

Know—may Allāh, His Messenger, and His *walī* guide us to what He loves and is pleased with—that the stingy will never enter the Divine Assembly of the Most Glorious. Likewise, understand that those who show off are expelled from the Mercy of the Most Merciful by their very own good deeds.

Herein lies the secret of giving: you should give from your wealth, your self, and your time without following it with reminders of your generosity and causing harm. Allāh, the Exalted, says: **A kind word and forgiveness are better than charity followed by harm. And Allāh is Free of need and Forbearing.**[51]

First and foremost, the seeker should understand that the *walī* is self-sufficient through Allāh, while everyone else is in need of him due to their distance from Allāh. It must also be known that the *walī* is

....

51   *Sūra 2. Al Baqara, verse 263.*

unaffected by the wealth of Qārūn (Korah) or the palaces of Pharaoh. He is the one who, by Allāh's command, sustains this universe—a universe that was brought from non-existence into existence only through the secret of the Prophet and his noble family, peace and blessings be upon them.

Sayyidunā ʿAlī—may Allāh honor his face—asked: "O Messenger of Allāh, from what were you created?" The Prophet ﷺ bowed his head for a while, then raised it with sweat like pearls on his forehead, and said: "O ʿAlī, when I was taken up to the heavens and was as close to my Lord as two bow-lengths or nearer, I asked, 'O my Lord, from what was I created?' He said, 'O Muḥammad, by My glory and majesty, if it were not for you, I would not have created My Paradise or My Hell.' I asked, 'O my Lord, from what was I created?' He said, 'When I looked at the purity of the whiteness of My Light, which I created by My power and perfected by My wisdom, and to which I added honor by associating it with My greatness, I extracted a part of it and divided it into three parts. From the first part, I created you and your family; from the second part, I created your wives and companions; and from the third part, I created those who love you. When the Day of Judgment comes, each group will return to its origin and lineage, and I will return that light to My Light. Then I will admit you, your family, your companions, and those who love you into My Paradise by My mercy. So, inform them of this, O Muḥammad, on My behalf.'"[52]

Ibn 'Asākir narrated from Sayyidunā Salmān al-Fārsī—may Allāh be pleased with him—that the Prophet ﷺ said: "Gabriel—peace be upon him—descended and said: 'O Muḥammad, your Lord says to you: If I took Abraham as a friend, then I have taken you as My beloved, and I have not created any creature more honorable to Me than you. I created the world and its inhabitants to make known to them your honor and status with Me. Were it not for you, I would not have created the world.'"[53]

It is sufficient for you to know that the *walī* hears, sees, seizes, prays, and seeks refuge through Allāh. Do not think you are doing him a favor by giving, and do not imagine that you have added anything to him. He is enriched by Allāh, not by you. It is better for you and me to understand that whatever we have been granted the success to give on this path, it is only to free ourselves from the prison of our own oppression.

Therefore, if a seeker has wealth that he wishes to give, he should not inform anyone except his teacher, so that his illusory self does not deceive him before

....

52 Imām al-Suyūṭī, *Al-Durr al-Munazzam.*
53 Al-Suyuti, *Al-Durr al-Manthur,* Vol. 1, p. 61.

his peers, and their praise does not ruin the sincerity of his good deeds. The seeker should also know that if he wishes to help his brother on the path with money, he should approach his Shaykh, give it to him, and ask him to conceal his gift. This way, his needy brother's attitude towards him will not change, and he will not be esteemed more than his fellow seekers who do not have wealth.

A. The One-Fifth (*al-khumus*)

Know—and Allāh and His *walī* are higher and more knowledgeable—that the Prophet's family, according to the explicit text of the *ḥadīth*, inherit from the Prophet ﷺ certain rights, as he left them among us. By the clear text of the Qur'ān, they are entitled to the one-fifth (*khumus*) of the spoils and wealth.

Allāh, the Exalted, says in *Sūra* Al-Anfāl: **And know that anything you obtain of war booty—then indeed, for Allāh is one fifth of it and for the Messenger and for [his] near relatives and the orphans, the needy, and the [stranded] traveler, if you have believed in Allāh and in that which We sent down to Our Servant on the day of criterion—the day when the two armies met. And Allāh, over all things, is competent.**[54]

....

54 *Sūra* 8. *Al-Anfāl*, verse 41.

So whoever wishes to follow the path should refrain from withholding and offer one-fifth of whatever his hands gain to the descendants of the Prophet, peace and blessings be upon him. This is the foundation for achieving closeness, knowledge, and blessings in all aspects, both foundational and peripheral. For the one who offers it, all goodness will accompany him on the path of blessings, while the one who neglects it will find the sources of his connection dried up in all his actions.

And never think that the Shaykh—may Allāh sanctify his noble secret—will ask you for it, for he is noble and pure, and asks only from Allāh. Be wise and discerning, and do not assume that your lower self and its companion, al-Qarīn[55], will make the path of wisdom easy for you. Rather, you will find them burning within you until you abandon this deed, which strikes them down like a sword against an enemy.

B. The Gift (*al-hadiyya*)

Let the seeker understand that the highest form of giving is the gift a disciple presents to his Shaykh. The Prophet, peace and blessings be upon him, said that gifts strengthen love in hearts, and we are indeed in

....

55 A devil that is assigned to any human since his birth.

desperate need of a place in the heart of the Beloved of the Most Merciful. A gift offered to the Shaykh and his family, without reminding them of the favor (*tamannun*) and with a heart seeking only their satisfaction, becomes a source of tranquility, prayer, nearness, and protection from all harm. There is no form of giving on the path of Allāh that surpasses this. Also, know that giving to the son is akin to giving to his grandfather, peace and blessings be upon them. The Messenger of Allāh ﷺ said: "Exchange gifts, and you will love one another."[56]

He also said: "Love Allāh for the blessings with which He nourishes you, love me for the love of Allāh, and love my family for my love."[57]

And Aisha, may Allāh be pleased with her, said: "The Messenger of Allāh ﷺ would accept gifts and reward for them."[58]

The reward of the Prophet ﷺ is his love and the blessing of his supplication, and establishing a connection with him and finding tranquility is found in the presence of his inheritor in one's time, peace

....

56 Al-Bukhārī, *Al-Adab Al-Mufrad, Bāb al-Hadiyya* (Chapter on Gifts), *ḥadīth* No. 594.

57 Al-Tirmidhī, *Sunan al-Tirmidhī, Kitāb al-Manāqib* (*The Book of Virtues*), *ḥadīth* No. 3789.

58 Al-Bukhārī, *Ṣaḥīḥ al-Bukhārī, Kitāb al-Hibah* (*The Book of Gifts*), *ḥadīth* No. 2585.

and blessings be upon both of them. Among the etiquettes of giving a gift is that it should always be one of the most precious and beloved items to the giver. You should not visit your Shaykh without bringing such a gift. Mawlānā Shaykh—may Allāh sanctify his noble secret—narrates to us that one of the saints of the past would not accept a disciple in his circle unless the disciple brought a gift each time he joined, even though Allāh Almighty had bestowed upon him great wealth. When one of his disciples asked about this practice in his method of education, he replied: "You have to spend from what is most valuable to you (meaning the worldly life—*dunyā*) so that we may spend from what is most valuable to us, which is the knowledge of Allāh."

And know that it is not recommended to exchange gifts among seekers, as this can stir the ego, whether through greed, arrogance, or vanity, creating spiritual diseases in the heart and building barriers (*fawāṣil*) on the straight path of Allāh.

C. Charity (*al-ṣadaqa*)

Know that the Shaykh—may Allāh sanctify his noble secret—is a descendant of the Prophet ﷺ and does not accept the impurities of people in the form of charity; he is pure, and he is a purificator. As he tells us—may Allāh sanctify his noble secret accept ing *ṣadaqa* for the Ahl al-Bayt (the family of the Prophet), peace be upon them, is more displeasing to Allāh than committing adultery. Therefore, never harbor the intention of giving *ṣadaqa* to your master, peace be upon him. He knows what is hidden in your heart, and if he takes it from you, he will not use it for himself, his family, or his wealth.

Abū Hurayra—may Allāh be pleased with him—narrated: "The Messenger of Allāh ﷺ would accept *hadiyya*, but he would not eat *ṣadaqa*."[59]

'Abd al-Muṭṭalib ibn Rabī'a ibn al-Ḥārith reported that the Prophet ﷺ said: "Ṣadaqa is not appropriate for the family of Muḥammad. It is the impurities of people, and it is not lawful for Muḥammad or the family of Muḥammad."[60]

If a seeker wishes to give *ṣadaqa*, he should not think that these *ḥadīths* mean he should refrain from doing so through the Shaykh—may Allāh sanctify his noble secret. Rather, it is better for him to give his *ṣadaqa*, *zakāt*, and all his wealth through his guide, so that he may fulfill the words of Allāh, the Exalted: **Take, [O Muḥammad], from their wealth a ṣadaqa**

....

59 Al-Bukhārī, *Ṣaḥīḥ al-Bukhārī*, *Kitāb al-Hibah* (*The Book of Gifts*), *ḥadīth* No. 2585.

60 Muslim, *Ṣaḥīḥ Muslim*, *Kitāb al-Zakāt* (*The Book of Charity*), *ḥadīth* No. 1069.

by which you purify them and cause them increase, and invoke [Allāh's blessings] upon them. Indeed, your invocations are reassurance for them. And Allāh is Hearing and Knowing.[61]

Whoever gives ṣadaqa through the medium of the *walī* will have it purified and blessed, establishing a connection to the Prophet, peace and blessings be upon him, and to the Lord of Glory, Allāh. This connection provides a secure refuge from the grasp of the lower world (*dunyā*) and its hardships. The most virtuous ṣadaqa and zakāt are those directed towards the *zāwiya* and its needs. However, if *ṣadaqa* is given without the intermediary of the Shaykh—may Allāh sanctify his noble secret—one may still be rewarded, but will not attain the deeper gifts of knowledge (*maʿrifa*), connection (*ṣila*), refinement (*tazkiya*), purification (*ṭahāra*), or tranquility (*sakīna*) unless Allāh wills otherwise. Indeed, Allāh does as He wills, and Allāh, His Messenger, and His walī are higher and more knowledgeable.

....

61 *Sūra* 9. *At-Tawba*, verse 103.

D. The Ransom (*fidya*)

Allāh the Exalted says in His Holy Book: **So today no ransom will be accepted from you or from those who disbelieved. Your refuge is the Fire; it is most worthy of you, and wretched is the destination.**[62]

Whoever wishes to protect himself from the fire of distance (*bu'd*) should offer a *fidya* from his wealth before his time runs out. And whoever seeks a good outcome should similarly offer whatever Allāh wills from his wealth in the form of a *fidya*. For any deed whose blessing you seek, any sin you wish to erase, or any trial you wish to alleviate, offer a *fidya* for it in this world, by passing it through the medium of the inheritor of the Prophet—peace and blessings be upon both of them. Allāh the Exalted says: **O you who have believed, when you privately consult (supplicate) the Messenger, present before your consultation (supplication) a *ṣadaqa*. That is better for you and purer. But if you do not find [the means], then indeed, Allāh is Forgiving and Merciful.**[63]

If you offer a *fidya* through the inheritor, you have done so through the one from whom the inheritance stems, peace be upon him, making your supplication closer to reaching Allāh. This act will carry all

....

62 Sūra 57. *Al-Ḥadīd*, verse 15.
63 Sūra 58. *Al-Mujādila*, verse 12.

the goodness you seek and be purer than presenting it with your own tainted hand. The reason is that the inheritor—may Allāh sanctify his noble secret—knows precisely where to place it for you. He will give it to the pious believers, whose prayers for you will ascend immediately. This is because the pious believer has realized himself in one of the Names of Allāh, "*al-Mu'min*" (The Faithful). When they partake of your *fidya*, the trace of the Name manifests in the apparent realm, connecting you directly to the Supreme Name "Allāh," as all the Names are annihilated within it.

The Messenger of Allāh ﷺ said: "Take no companion except a believer, and let no one eat your food except a God-conscious person (*taqī*)."[64]

. . . .

64 Abū Dāwūd, *Sunan Abī Dāwūd, Kitāb al-Adāb* (*The Book of Manners*), *ḥadīth* No. 4832.

VI.
The Virtues of Proper Etiquette
with the Keys of Majesty (*mafātīh al-jalāla*)

A. The Virtues of Proper Etiquette with the Light of Majesty and the Warning against Disrespecting it during *Mushāhada*

Know—and Allāh, His Messenger, and His walī are higher and more knowledgeable—that Allāh states in His Holy Book: **Allāh is Light.**[65] Therefore, His attribute never departs from His essence. Whoever witnesses the exemplification of the attribute witnesses the attribute itself, and whoever witnesses the attribute knocks on the door of the essence. Based on this, the people of Allāh have said that the highest degrees of proximity and knowledge are attained when Allāh's light manifests upon the seeker. It is narrated that Sayyidunā Abū Dharr al-Ghifārī—may Allāh be pleased with him—asked the Messenger of

....

65 *Sura 24. Al-Nur,* verse 35.

Allāh ﷻ: "Did you see your Lord?" He replied, "Light; I see Him!"[66] And he also said, "I saw Light."[67]

A particle of light from the holy radiance of His Face is more precious and greater than you, me, and all the worlds, forms, and nations that have existed and those yet to appear. Indeed, everything is in need of His light, as explicitly mentioned in the Qur'ān: **Allāh is the Light of the heavens and the earth.** But His light is in need of nothing—not you, not me, nor anything else. It is an attribute that Allāh, the Exalted, made self-sufficient through His own essence.

Therefore, whoever is granted a glimpse of this attribute's exemplification, even for a moment, and belittles it, in reality, magnifies his own thingness (*shay'iyya*), his transience (*fanā'*), his annihilation (*halāk*), and his misery (*balā'*). Such a person sanctifies his illusory reflection and rejects the original light. We seek refuge in Allāh from this manifest deviation. By doing so, he establishes arrogance within himself, distances himself from the circle of divine election (*iṣtifā'*), and closes off the gateway leading to the abode of permanence (*baqā'*).

This is a trap that we, the seekers of this misguided

....

66 Ibn al-Qayyim al-Jawziyya, *Zād al-Ma'ād*, Vol. 3, p. 33.
67 Muslim, *Ṣaḥīḥ Muslim, Kitāb al-Īmān* (*The Book of Faith*), *ḥadīth* No. 291.

age, often fall into due to the density of our souls and our obsessive sanctification of forms over reality. You will find that when a seeker witnesses a radiant, star-like light emanating from the Lord manifesting upon him, he belittles and disrespects it. Yet, if he sees a bearded man in white, it remains imprinted in his imagination with great reverence.

This is why most of us are not enveloped by His sacred light, which transcends directions and opposites (*aḍdād*), and why this light does not purify our souls filled with the love of lower desires. Light is exalted, and nothing surpasses it; if you dare to belittle or disrespect it, it will distance itself from you, not draw you closer.

It is better for the seeker, at the beginning of the path, to firmly implant in his mind—through self-convincing, striving (*mujāhada*), and humility—that light is the Lord of manifestations, with no partner in the realm of divine openings. If even a brief ray of light appears to him in his state of distance and lack of reverence, he should magnify it and humble himself before it. This is so the light may envelop him by Allāh's grace and through the share granted to him by the walī, may Allāh sanctify his secret.

The closest path to this sanctification is for the seeker to realize that the light is, in essence, his Shaykh, then his Messenger ﷺ, and ultimately Allāh

Almighty. The light is a reality that simultaneously brought together transcendence, as Allāh says: **Allāh is Light,** and its descent through its various degrees (*marātib*), from transcendence (*tanzīh*) to comparability (*tashbīh*), as Allāh says: **The exemplification of His light is like a niche within which is a lamp—the lamp is within a glass, the glass as if it were a shining star.**

Jābir ibn 'Abdullāh—may Allāh be pleased with him—said: I asked, "O Messenger of Allāh, may my father and mother be sacrificed for you, tell me about the first thing Allāh created before everything else." He ﷺ replied, "O Jābir, Allāh created, before all things, the light of your Prophet from His Light. He created it from His Light and added it to Himself, honoring it. He then made this light revolve and move in the realm of dominion (*malakūt*) by His power as He willed. At that time, there was no Tablet, no Pen, no Paradise, no Fire, no Angel, no heaven, no earth, no sun, no moon, no jinn, and no human. When Allāh willed to create the creation, He divided that light into four parts: from the first part, He created the Pen; from the second part, He created the Tablet; from the third part, He created the Throne. He then divided the fourth part into four portions: from the first, He created the bearers of the Throne; from the second, He created the *Kursī* (pedestal); from the third, He created the rest of the angels. He then divided the fourth portion into four parts: from the first, He created the heavens; from the second, He created the earth; from the third, He created Paradise and Hell. He then divided the fourth portion into four parts: from the first, He created the light of the believers' sight; from the second, He created the light of their hearts, which is knowledge of Allāh; and from the third, He created the light of their souls, which is the declaration that there is no deity but Allāh, and Muḥammad is the Messenger of Allāh."[68]

Thus, beware of any thought that suggests to you that the light is merely a visual reflection, illusion, or magic—may Allāh protect us from disbelief after faith. Do not tell the Shaykh—may Allāh sanctify his noble secret—that you do not see the light, for it does not envelop your vision due to your distance, the impurity of your past, your lack of submission, and your bad character. Your Shaykh, by virtue of his high standing with the Reckoner, will tear away seventy veils of darkness for you and open a door that looks into the niche of the Chosen One ﷺ, even if you are the most foolish of the two weighty creations (humankind and jinn).

....

68 Abd al-Razzāq al-Ṣanʿānī, *Jannat al-Khuld.*

Indeed, there is no disciple who recites the litanies of the path without witnessing this light; if he is not enveloped by the sun of his Shaykh's reality, then he is with his moon; if not his moon, then with his star; if not his star, then with its reflection in the stars in the niche; and if not, then with the rays of these stars from behind the clouds. Therefore, do not dare to deny the mercy that your Lord has bestowed upon you through the hand of your Shaykh, thereby expelling yourself from it with your own tongue.

When the *walī* asks you about your visualization of the light of Allāh, he tests you by every description you give of the attribute of the Most Merciful. Humble yourself when describing the light, and magnify the attribute with the greatness it deserves, according to the one it reflects. Do not say, "I see a dot of light, O Shaykh," thereby making yourself significant and the light insignificant. Instead, say, "O my master, due to my distance from Allāh Almighty and the corruption of my soul with what is other than Him, I see the reality of my distance in the manifestation of the blessed, star-like light, and it appears to me as a dot. Far be it from any diminishment—it is the Great, and I am the one distant from its reality. In what has manifested to me in my witnessing (*mushāhada*), it resembles a star in the sky of a summer night without clouds—you see it from a distance as a dot that sparkles, but when you draw near to it, your size becomes insignificant in comparison to it."

Whoever does not humble himself before the light of Allāh and fails to carefully choose his words when describing it will find it difficult to bear the secrets of this light, unless the walī wills otherwise.

B. Do not Disclose the Prophet's Honor: The Innermost Secret

Know—and Allāh, His Messenger, and His walī are more exalted and more knowledgeable than you and I—that the path the walī arranges for you to know Allāh takes you through seventy secrets, all of which descend from the Holy Assembly of Divine Election (*ḥaḍrat al-iṣṭifa'*) and are reserved exclusively for the elite of the believers and the saints. The Prophet, peace and blessings be upon him, when gathered with the people of realization after the morning prayer, would close the door of the mosque and ask if there was a stranger among them. If there was, he would conceal from him the knowledge he could not bear, but if there was not, he would reveal the secrets of sincerity (*asrār al-ikhlāṣ*) to the chosen ones. The Messenger of Allāh ﷺ said: "Speak to people according to their understanding."

So beware of speaking to the common folk with the language of the elect, lest you destroy both them and yourself. Revealing the secrets of divinity is unanimously agreed upon as an act of disbelief (*kufr*), and the people of Allāh have described it as an assault—may Allāh protect us—on the honor of the best of creation, our master Muḥammad, peace and blessings be upon him. Likewise, do not speak to the elect about degrees of secrets they have not yet reached, or you will cut off the path for both them and yourself. Rather, speak to those at your level with the secret of Allāh, so that you may receive from them what has been hidden from you regarding the different facets of this secret. That said, it is always better to address your understanding to your Shaykh, who encompasses all the facets and all the paths leading to the knowledge of Allāh.

And know that a secret remains a secret even if you reveal it; it is transcendent and cannot be likened to anything, even if you create an orbit around it to exemplify it. Anyone who lacks the secret also lacks its orbits. If you try to draw an orbit of the secret for such a person, you will drown him in the swamps of analogy, for he has no foundation or source from which to inhale the breaths of monotheism. One who lacks access to the gate of transcendence and whom you attempt to speak with about Allāh will delimit every meaning you express by the constraints of what he perceives in terms of forms or rational concepts.

He will either create an idol in his mind that he calls God or deny anything that cannot be confined within his delimited understanding, reducing God to mere written words, incapable of embracing absolute existence beyond delimitation. When you illuminate such a person with a facet of the truth, he denies it, for truth is a secret that flows through both negation and affirmation, from the non-delimited within the delimited without delimitation. Therefore, speak to the common folk only through the clear guidance of the *sharīʿa*, and direct them solely towards the light of Allāh, for it is the gateway between all things, the *walī*, and Allāh.

Conclusion

Praise be to Allāh, by whose will righteous deeds are completed! O Allāh, make this work a light that descends morning and evening upon my mother, Essia, the light of my eyes, my father and master, Anouar, my brothers, Khaled and Marouen, my sister, Dorra, and all who have supported Mawlānā Shaykh—may Allāh sanctify his noble secret—by the honor of the Master of Messengers and all his family. Amen.

Printed and bound
in the United States of America